Close-up

WORKBOOK

B2

Katrina Gormley

SECOND EDITION

NATIONAL
GEOGRAPHIC
L E A R N I N G

Australia · Brazil · Mexico · Singapore · United Kingdom · United States

NATIONAL GEOGRAPHIC
L E A R N I N G

Close-up B2 Workbook, Second Edition
Katrina Gormley

Publisher: Sue Trory

Development Editor: Kayleigh Buller

Editorial Assistant: Georgina McComb

Text/Cover Designer: Ken Vail Graphic Design

Content Project Manager: Cathy Reay

Editorial Liaison: Leila Hishmeh

For product information and technology assistance, contact us at
Cengage Learning Customer & Sales Support, cengage.com/contact

For permission to use material from this text or product,
submit all requests online at **cengage.com/permissions**
Further permissions questions can be emailed to
permissionrequest@cengage.com

ISBN: 978-1-4080-9574-4

National Geographic Learning
Cheriton House, North Way, Andover, Hampshire, SP10 5BE
United Kingdom

National Geographic Learning, a Cengage Learning Company, has a mission to bring the world to the classroom and the classroom to life. With our English language programs, students learn about their world by experiencing it. Through our partnerships with National Geographic and TED Talks, they develop the language and skills they need to be successful global citizens and leaders.

Locate your local office at **international.cengage.com/region**

Visit National Geographic Learning online at **NGL.Cengage.com/ELT**
Visit our corporate website at **www.cengage.com**

Photo credits

Cover images: (front cover) © WLADIMIR BULGAR/Science Photo Library/Corbis, (back cover) © Paul Sampson/Alamy

4–31 (all) shutterstock, **32** (cr) World History Archive/Image Asset Management Ltd/Alamy, **32–69** (all) shutterstock, **71** Jamie Grill/Tetra Images/Alamy, **72–87** (all) shutterstock.

Illustrations: Illustrations by Panagiotis Angeletakis

The publisher has made every effort to trace and contact copyright holders before publication. If any have been inadvertently overlooked, the publisher will be pleased to rectify any errors or omissions at the earliest opportunity.

Printed in the United Kingdom by Ashford Colour Press Ltd.
Print Number: 20   Print Year: 2024

Contents

Reading

A Read the *Exam Reminder*. What should you do first?

_____

B Now complete the *Exam Task*.

Exam Reminder

Identifying key information
- With multiple-choice sentences, remember to read the sentence stems first and underline the key words.
- Try to find the section of the text that matches the underlined key words.
- Don't forget to read the answer options carefully before matching to the text. Then you underline the correct answer.

How to be a teenager and survive!

Being a teenager in these troubled times isn't exactly a walk in the park. The uncertainty only adds to the typical list of problems you're already facing. So, what are the challenges you are up against and how can you weather the storm and arrive safely on the other side?

As a teenager, the biggest challenge you, your family and friends face is mood swings. One minute you feel ecstatic, full of confidence and optimism and the next you feel depressed, angry at the world and certain that you are a failure. Personal appearance also becomes a huge issue. The hormones racing through your body play havoc with your self-image. Suddenly, you have become too fat, too thin, too ugly, too short, too tall; your hair is too dark, too light, too curly, too straight, etc. In short, you are completely dissatisfied with your appearance.

Relationships with others also become more complicated. You may find you no longer have that much in common with the friends you've been hanging around with for years. It can also be distressing when a former best friend now prefers to spend time with other friends. As for family relationships, well, it often seems that a war has been declared, and parents and siblings have become the enemy.

But it needn't all be doom and gloom. The teenage years are **unique** in a person's life. They mark the end of childhood and the important passage to adulthood. The key to a happy 'teenhood' is to recognise that no matter how your emotions change or how insecure you feel about yourself, you are perfectly normal! Everyone, big and small, experiences feelings of depression and anxiety from time to time. But here are a few tips to help you get through your darkest moments.

Communication has got to be the first tip. If you keep negative feelings in, you'll reach a point where you think you're going to explode. Confide in someone about how you are feeling with someone you can trust. Even if they can't give you the advice you need, just getting it off your chest can make a world of difference.

But, what can you do if you're at exploding point and there's no one to talk to? If you want to avoid conflict with others, go somewhere on your own for a minute or two to process things. Take time to breathe properly. When we are in stressful situations our breathing becomes short and rushed, and as a result less oxygen reaches the brain. This can heighten negative feelings that we have. One technique is to close one nostril with your thumb and inhale, then close the other nostril with your index finger and exhale as you release your thumb from the first nostril. Do this at least ten times and your breathing will return to normal and you will feel much calmer in next to no time.

Physical exercise like running, cycling and swimming are also great ways to clear the mind and they have the added bonus of keeping you fit. If you do this whenever you're down, you'll also start to feel better about yourself and your body. There's no need to push yourself to the limits, though. Listen to your body and stop when it says, 'No more!'

Finally, always try to focus on the positive aspects of your life. Being a teenager means you have more freedom. Use it in constructive ways so that feelings of frustration are replaced by feelings of accomplishment.

You are going to read an article on how to survive as a teenager. For question **1 – 6** choose the answer (**a, b, c** or **d**) which you think fits best according to the text.

1 As a result of the current world situation,
  a everyone has the same problems.
  b teenagers are coping better than others.
  c people feel insecure about the future.
  d the problems confronting teenagers have changed completely.

2 Teenagers often have to deal with
  a sudden emotional changes.
  b the anger of relatives and friends.
  c constantly putting on and losing weight.
  d lack of success.

3 During the teenage years,
  a family members always stop talking to one another.
  b hormonal changes can make young people dissatisfied with how they look.
  c best friends always grow apart.
  d personal appearance becomes the most important aspect of a teenager's life.

4 What does the word '**unique**' in paragraph 4 tell us about the teen years?
  a They cause a lot of anxiety.
  b They are a very special time in our lives.
  c All teenagers experience them in the same way.
  d Teenagers ought to be happier.

5 According to the writer, angry teenagers feel better
  a by listening to the advice of others.
  b by bottling up their feelings.
  c by talking about their feelings.
  d by taking short, quick breaths.

6 The writer encourages teenagers to
  a respect their body and its limitations.
  b exercise only when they are depressed.
  c ask their parents for more freedom.
  d take up a competitive sport.

Vocabulary

A Read the *Exam Reminder*. What should you check?
_____

B Now complete the *Exam Task*.

Exam Task

Complete the sentences with the correct form of the words in capitals.

1 Jan is so _____ with her new job that she's thinking of leaving. **SATISFY**

2 Many people who live alone suffer from _____. **ALONE**

3 The meal he prepared was so _____ no one could eat it!. **DISGUST**

4 Tania's very bright, but she lacks _____. **CONFIDENT**

5 Are you very _____ about your exam results? **ANXIETY**

6 She was so _____ in her new job, she didn't mind working at weekends. **HAPPINESS**

Exam Reminder

Transforming words

- Try to create a word family for each word given in the task.
- Remember to think about which form (noun, adjective or adverb) would fit best in the sentence.
- Don't forget you must always check the spelling of the words you write. You will lose marks for words spelled incorrectly.

C Match the first parts of the sentences 1–6 to the second parts a–f.

1 The player limped in ☐
2 All the way through the play, she was on ☐
3 When I heard about the break-up, I was at ☐
4 Seeing the huge flames, James ran out of the office in ☐
5 I haven't been on ☐
6 Don't let Fiona get under ☐

  a a loss for words.
  b good terms with my boss since last December.
  c your skin; she's just insecure.
  d the edge of her seat.
  e agony off the field.
  f a panic.

D Complete the words in the sentences.

1 A phobia is an i _ _ _ _ _ _ _ _ fear of something specific.
2 Never be afraid to e _ _ _ _ _ _ your feelings.
3 I was a _ _ _ _ _ to find out they were getting married.

4 How will the new changes a _ _ _ _ your job?
5 What a s _ _ _ _ you missed the party!
6 I've been feeling m _ _ _ _ _ _ _ _ all day

Grammar

Present Simple & Present Continuous

A Find and correct the mistakes in the sentences.

1 We are going to the beach every day. _____
2 Why are you complaining always about the weather? _____
3 These roses are smelling lovely. _____
4 They have a test usually at the end of each term. _____
5 Are neurons sending messages to the brain? _____
6 What do you stare at? _____
7 I look for the station. Can you tell me where it is? _____
8 She gets more and more excited about her birthday every day. _____

B Complete the sentences with the Present Simple or the Present Continuous form of these verbs.

belong burst into freak out go look not see show take take off

1 What time _____ the plane _____?
2 _____ this science book _____ to you?
3 The referee _____ Garibaldi a red card and the whole stadium _____ wild!
4 Every winter, we _____ skiing lessons.
5 Anne _____ miserable. Is anything wrong?
6 Sharon _____ always _____ tears during sad films.
7 My mum _____ when I stay out too late.
8 I _____ Sam anymore.

Listening

A Read the *Exam Reminder*. How many options should you choose for your answer?

_____

B 🔊 1.1 ▶ Now complete the *Exam Task*.

Exam Reminder

Highlighting key words

- Remember to read the multiple-choice questions, and identify who is talking and what they are talking about.
- It helps if you underline key words in the questions.
- Then, read all of the answer options and think about the meaning of each of the keywords. If you are having trouble understanding some words, try to think of other words that may mean the same thing.
- Don't forget that only one option will answer the question!

Exam Task

You will hear people talking in six different situations. For questions **1 – 6**, choose the best answer (**a, b or c**).

1 You hear a man talking about his family life. How does he feel?
   a free
   b lonely
   c anxious

2 You hear a mother talking to her son. Why is she talking to him?
   a to congratulate him
   b to calm him down
   c to give him some advice

3 You hear two teenagers talking. What is the girl dissatisfied with?
   a her appearance
   b her weight
   c her performance at school

4 You hear a man and a woman talking. Who is the man no longer on good terms with?
   a his brother
   b his sister-in-law
   c his children

5 You hear a man talking about flying. What did he dislike about it?
   a confined spaces
   b heights
   c being bored

6 You hear a woman talking on the radio. What is she?
   a a school teacher
   b an agony aunt
   c a writer

C 🔊 1.1 ▶ Listen again and check your answers.

Grammar

Present Perfect Simple & Present Perfect Continuous

A Complete the sentences using the Present Perfect Simple or the Present Perfect Continuous form of the verbs in brackets.

1 Why _____ you _____ (not clean) the bathroom yet?

2 The professor _____ (give) lectures all afternoon.

3 I _____ (never be) outside Europe.

4 The children _____ (just meet) their new cousin.

5 _____ Dora _____ (run)? Her face is bright red!

6 It's the first time Rob _____ (ask) me a favour.

7 Where _____ they _____ (stay) since they arrived in Madrid?

8 You _____ (not give) us enough time to complete the task.

B Complete the text with the Present Perfect Simple or the Present Perfect Continuous of these verbs.

> date end get give hit make meet part

Hugh Grant (**1**) _____ the headlines for decades with stories of his relationships with fellow stars. In the past, he (**2**) _____ celebrities such as Liz Hurley and Jemima Khan. The press (**3**) _____ often _____ him the nickname of the best-loved bachelor in show-biz. However, the actor (**4**) _____ recently _____ the latest love of his live: his newborn son whom he (**5**) _____ to know away from the public. Unfortunately, he (**6**) _____ it clear that his relationship with the baby's mother (**7**) _____. Nevertheless, they (**8**) _____ on good terms and Grant is said to be very supportive of her and their daughter.

Use your English

A For questions 1 – 6, complete the second sentence so that it has a similar meaning to the first sentence, using the word given. Do not change the word given. You must use between two and five words, including the word given.

1 We have never worked for a multinational company until now.
   first
   This _____ we have worked for a multinational company.

2 He boarded the plane at 4 pm and it's now 8 pm.
   travelling
   He _____ on the plane for four hours.

3 I have never seen such a beautiful sunset.
   ever
   That is the most beautiful sunset _____ seen.

4 I didn't know what to say when they told me the news.
   loss
   I _____ words when they told me the news.

5 This is my first trip to Paris.
   never
   I _____ to Paris before.

6 I met Sue at university.
   since
   I _____ we were at university.

B Read the *Exam Reminder*. What should you be careful about?

_____

C Now complete the *Exam Task*.

Exam Reminder

Completing gapped texts

- It's a good idea to read the text first to get the general idea of it.
- Then look carefully at what comes before and after each gap.
- Remember to decide what type of word is missing.
- Don't forget to finally read the text again when complete to make sure it all makes sense.

Exam Task

For questions 1 – 10, read the text below and think of the word which best fits each gap. Use only one word in each gap.

What does your facial expression say about you?

People often say that the eyes are a window to the soul and the face is a mirror of our emotions. We can often predict how someone will react (1) _____ certain situations by watching their facial expressions. If someone is (2) _____ a loss for words, for example, their eyebrows will usually move upwards and their mouth may open slightly. Also, fury (3) _____ another emotion which is hard for someone to hide. Again the eyebrows are important – an angry face will have knitted eyebrows, the mouth will be closed tightly while the nostrils may flare open. At the other end of the spectrum, a broad smile and shining eyes reveal a person's (4) _____. Happiness is an emotion which is easily detected by looking at the face. There are times, however, when people need to hide their emotions. They may be in a situation where it would be uncomfortable (5) _____ inconvenient for other people to know how they are feeling. For example, in a class full of students, a teacher may (6) _____ like bursting into tears, but this would usually be inappropriate. He or she may try to cover up this emotion by faking a smile. For this reason, some psychologists believe that the face alone isn't capable of (7) _____ how we truly feel. Instead it is only one of several factors that we can base assumptions (8) _____ about how someone is feeling. Recent research has helped psychologists such as Paul Eckman gain even more (9) _____ about how we interpret facial expressions and come to conclusions about other people's emotions. Studies with subjects from different cultures have shown (10) _____ that tone of voice and overall body language also provide us with valuable clues.

writing: an informal email / letter

A Read the writing task below and answer the questions.

You have received an email from your English-speaking friend, Joy, who has been having some problems with her best friend. Read Joy's email and the notes you have made. Then write an email to Joy, using all your notes.

Learning Reminder

Using the correct tone

- Remember to use the language that shows the correct tone.
- Try to start your email with a friendly greeting and sign off in an appropriate way.
- Don't forget to keep the tone friendly and chatty.
- It helps to consider staging and sequencing when writing any email.
- Remember to cover all notes from the email in your reply.

mailbox

Reply | Reply All | Forward | Delete

From: Joy Summers   **Date:** 1st August   **Subject:** Help!

Hi Clara,

I haven't seen you in ages! I saw your sister at Jack's birthday party last weekend. Why didn't you come too?   → Explain

It's a pity, because I had been really looking forward to seeing you and having a good chat.

The party was absolutely fab, but unfortunately, I spilt a drink on Kate's new white dress and she was furious with me.   → Ask for more details

She still won't speak to me! Can you believe it! It's really upsetting as we've been best friends since primary school and we've never fallen out before. How can I get her to forgive me?   → Suggest

By the way, I took masses of photos at the party. Do you want me to send you some?
→ No, because ...

Reply soon,
Joy

Write your **email** in 140–190 words in an appropriate style.

1 What should Clara give an explanation for in her reply?

2 What should Clara ask more details about?

3 What suggestion should Clara make?

4 What will Clara say 'No' to?

5 Why do you think she might say 'No'?

B Read the model email and circle exclamation marks, underline abbreviations and highlight friendly expressions in the beginning and when signing off.

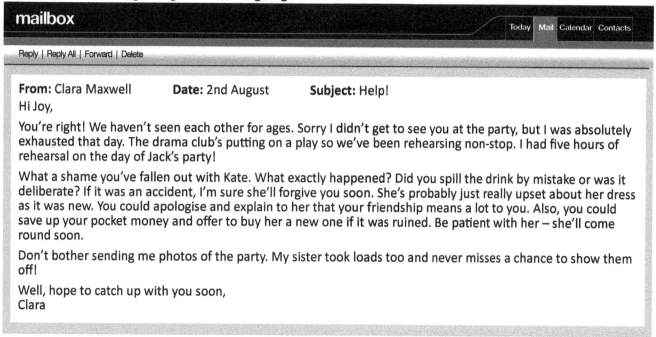

mailbox

Today | Mail | Calendar | Contacts

Reply | Reply All | Forward | Delete

From: Clara Maxwell   **Date:** 2nd August   **Subject:** Help!

Hi Joy,

You're right! We haven't seen each other for ages. Sorry I didn't get to see you at the party, but I was absolutely exhausted that day. The drama club's putting on a play so we've been rehearsing non-stop. I had five hours of rehearsal on the day of Jack's party!

What a shame you've fallen out with Kate. What exactly happened? Did you spill the drink by mistake or was it deliberate? If it was an accident, I'm sure she'll forgive you soon. She's probably just really upset about her dress as it was new. You could apologise and explain to her that your friendship means a lot to you. Also, you could save up your pocket money and offer to buy her a new one if it was ruined. Be patient with her – she'll come round soon.

Don't bother sending me photos of the party. My sister took loads too and never misses a chance to show them off!

Well, hope to catch up with you soon,
Clara

C Read and complete the *Exam Task* below. Don't forget to use the *Useful Expressions* on page 15 of your Student's Book.

Exam Task

You have received an email from your English-speaking friend, Aidan, whose birthday is next week. Read Aidan's email and the notes you have made. Then write an email to Aidan, using all your notes.

mailbox

Today | Mail | Calendar | Contacts

Reply | Reply All | Forward | Delete

Hi,

What have you been up to lately? I heard you've joined a football team. How's that going? → *Give details*

I don't know if you've heard, but it's my birthday next week and I'm planning to do something special on that day. → *Explain how you found out*

The thing is, I'm not sure what to arrange. One idea is to have a barbecue in our garden, though it would mean my dad would have to be there to help us out. Mum suggested inviting a small group of friends and taking them to the cinema and then maybe for pizza. What do you think? → *Suggest*

Oh, I nearly forgot. We're going camping this weekend, but I don't have a sleeping bag. Could I borrow yours? → *No, because ...*

Speak to you soon,

Aidan

Write your **email** in 140–190 words in an appropriate style.

→ Writing Reference p. 178 in Student's Book

2 One World?

Reading

A Read the *Exam Reminder*. What should you do before reading the article?

_____

B Now complete the *Exam Task*.

Exam Reminder

Finding similar words and phrases in the text

- Remember to read the matching questions first and underline the key words in each before reading the text.
- Try to read the article quickly, looking for words and phrases which link to the key words you underlined in the questions.
- It helps if you take one question at a time.

GLOBAL VERSUS LOCAL

Globalisation is a fact of modern life. We asked four very different people to talk to us about globalisation in their lives.

A Matt Townsend, IT director

I work for a large multinational corporation, so doing business on a global level and co-operating with colleagues around the world is part and parcel of the job. It's fascinating how international teams of people can communicate with each other and work together to reach common goals and make bigger profits. It's not always plain sailing, though, as sometimes cultural differences can cause misunderstandings. That's why it's so important that executives travel regularly to other countries in which we have offices. That way we can get to know each other better and understand how people in different countries think and operate. Personally, I love travelling and coming into contact with new cultures. Although to be perfectly honest, most of the time we hardly ever venture outside the hotels we're staying in. It's really our local colleagues in each destination that give us a taste of what life is like in their country.

B Jan Cooper, MP

Over the past century, we have certainly witnessed a boom in globalisation. International trading has become a fact of life, and as consumers we have become more demanding because we now expect to be able to buy the same products as residents of foreign countries. Also, as tourists we expect to find the products we usually buy at home when we travel abroad. However, the current economic crisis, which is crippling Western societies, has meant that we need to protect our own economies. The word on most MPs' lips these days is 'localisation'. It seems to make sense that, given the state of local economies, people should consume goods that have been made in their own country. We all have to make a bigger effort to buy closer to the source in order to support local producers and manufacturers and not dwelling on cultural boundaries. That way, more jobs will be created in our region and the economy will benefit.

C Anne Banks, Founder of Horizons Global School

I've always been a keen traveller, so when my daughter was born I began to think of solutions for combining travelling with bringing up a child. So, we set up Horizons. It's a global school because students here come from all over the world and each term they study in a different country. We partner with private international schools in each country we operate in. The idea is that students learn about the world by seeing and experiencing the sights, smells and tastes of the countries that make it up. One of the subjects they study is Global Culture. This term, they're in Vienna, so in Global Culture they will concentrate on how the people of Vienna live on a day-to-day basis. They'll examine the similarities and differences of Vienna in relation to other cities they studied in during previous terms. Students at the school certainly broaden their horizons in ways that wouldn't be possible if they went to their local school, which in turn will lead to more tolerance.

D Ron Carlton, Football player

I come from a long line of football players: my great-grandfather, my grandfather and my dad all played for our local club. That's what you did back then. You supported your local team and, if you were lucky and talented enough, you got to play for your local team. But not nowadays. I started my career at my local football club, but I was soon snapped up by a talent scout for a French team. I was only seventeen when I signed my first contract with them. It was a bit scary at first, being so young, but I soon got used to it and even picked up a bit of French. I also learnt the lyrics to some French songs! Three years later, I found myself in Italy. That was hard to get used to. I found it really difficult to adjust there. Even on the pitch it was hard. The players there have got a completely different mentality. I only stuck it out for one season. It was a bit of a relief when I signed a contract which brought me back to Wales. I'm thoroughly enjoying being back on native soil and I'm not planning to move in the foreseeable future.

You are going to read an article about globalisation. For questions **1 – 8**, choose from the people (**A – D**). The people may be chosen more than once.

Which person

1 finds it fascinating how international teams manage to communicate? ☐

2 has a suggestion for improving life in his/her own country? ☐

3 is someone who prefers his/her own country? ☐

4 talks about an unusual approach to education? ☐

5 loves travelling and wants to offer new cultural experiences to young people? ☐

6 wants a move away from Globalisation? ☐

7 has experienced problems due to cultural differences? ☐

8 is a person who travels on a regular basis? ☐

Vocabulary

A Choose the correct words.

1 Harry works for a multinational society / company.

2 We can exchange / expand information with foreign colleagues at the international conference.

3 Mum and Dad want us to move / spread to another country.

4 Jade lives on a houseboat on a canal / port.

5 The aspects / lifestyles of the rich and famous differ from those of other people.

6 The *Titanic* departed / traded from Southampton.

B Complete the sentences with these words.

concept   custom   influence   knowledge   phenomenon

1 Fire-jumping is a local _____ in some areas of Greece.

2 To the best of my _____, you don't need a passport on domestic flights.

3 Have you ever seen a strange natural _____ like the Northern Lights?

4 The _____ of the evil eye is popular in many countries.

5 Cleopatra had a strong _____ over her people.

C Read the *Exam Reminder*. What's the most important thing to look at before filling in the gap?

_____
_____

D Now complete the *Exam Task*. Use the words below to help you.

civilisation   national   Egyptian   global
American   occurrence   professional   beliefs

Exam Reminder

Looking at text around a gap

• Before completing a gapped text, remember to read the whole text first.

• It's very important to decide on what type of word is missing.

• Don't forget to think about what each gapped sentence means before choosing a word to complete it.

Exam Task

For questions **1 – 8**, read the text below and think of a word which best fits each gap. Use only **one** word in each gap.

Where East Meets West

The (**1**) _____ pyramids in Giza are shrouded in mystery. Well-known worldwide, the pyramids are a shining example of how the (**2**) _____ of ancient Egypt was very advanced. These wonderful constructions have made Giza a hotspot for (**3**) _____ tourism as people flock there from all over the world. However, just across the busy road that separates the archaeological site and the city, tourists are met with a strange sight: a popular (**4**) _____ fast-food restaurant.

This has become a common (**5**) _____ in many countries of the world. It would seem that (**6**) _____ business principles have taken over from local customs.

What is more, because these companies make sure their branches are almost identical, many people feel they are more (**7**) _____ and reliable than local companies. This means they are becoming more and more popular throughout the world. As a result, the customs, habits and even the (**8**) _____ of the local people are changing and becoming more westernised.

Grammar

Past Simple & Past Continuous; *Used to & Would*

A Circle the correct words.

1 We were travelling through India when the monsoon started / was starting.
2 My grandfather would / used to love reading about different cultures.
3 I was searching / searched for the passports, and Mary was counting our foreign currency.
4 They would go / were going snowboarding every winter.
5 Do you know who built / was building the Taj Mahal?
6 We got off the plane, we were collecting / collected our luggage and we left the airport.
7 Claire stayed / was staying in a hotel at the time of the earthquake.
8 I was watching / used to watch documentaries about ancient civilisations when I was young.

B Complete the sentences by writing one word in each gap.

1 Where did you _____ to go on holiday as a child?
2 Marion _____ packing her suitcase when I arrived.
3 _____ you learn a lot on the safari?
4 _____ the sausages that you ate in Germany spicy?
5 Every night, the campers _____ light a fire on the beach.
6 Gemma and Fay _____ making sushi, and Ryanne was preparing spring rolls.
7 _____ the train travelling at top speed when it was derailed?
8 They _____ not reach the summit in time.

C Answer the questions about yourself.

1 Where would you play as a child?
  _____
2 What were you doing this time yesterday?
  _____
3 How often did you use to go on holiday as a child?
  _____
4 Where were you living in 2003?
  _____
5 What foods did you not use to eat that you eat now?
  _____
6 When was the last time you boarded a ship?
  _____

Listening

A Read the *Exam Reminder*. What do you have to try to predict?

_____

B Listen and complete the *Exam Task*.

Exam Reminder

Predicting content

- Remember to look at the gaps to try to predict what type of word is missing.
- Read the gapped sentences and underline the key words. Remember that they are usually just before or just after the gaps.
- Try to listen carefully and then write your answers.
- Don't forget to read the text again with your answers in place to check it makes sense.

Exam Task

2.1 You will hear an interview with Laura Modini, a student at Horizons Global School. For questions 1 – 7, complete the sentences with a word or short phrase.

1 At present, Laura Modini is studying in _____.
2 Students at Horizons change country and go to a _____ each term.
3 This is Laura's _____ studying at the global school.
4 Melbourne has got a great _____ so people can get around easily.
5 Laura found it easier to get to know Belfast and Amsterdam because they are both _____ cities.
6 Laura says she's _____ to be a student at Horizons.
7 Global Culture helps students to understand local _____.

C **2.1** Listen again and check your answers.

Grammar

Past Simple vs Present Perfect Simple

A Complete the text with the Past Simple or the Present Perfect Simple form of these verbs.

> be   do   enjoy   fly   have   have   spend   visit

Lily: I'm thinking about going to France in the autumn.
(1) _____ you ever _____ there?

Tod: Yes! In fact, my sister and I (2) _____ back from Paris last week. We (3) _____ ten wonderful days there. I (4) _____ never _____ so much fun before on holiday.

Lily: What (5) _____ you _____ there?

Tod: Well, we (6) _____ all the popular tourist sights like the Eiffel Tower, the Louvre and of course, Eurodisney!

Lily: Aren't you a bit old for that?

Tod: Not at all! It's the first time my sister and I (7) _____ ourselves so much. We (8) _____ a go on almost all the rides there. If you go to France, don't miss it.

B Find and circle the ten mistakes in the text below.

When the group has set out for the mountains that morning, they didn't realise what an ordeal lay ahead of them. They have planned to be back before dusk and asked the inn-keeper to prepare an evening meal for them. The idea was to walk up to the highest peak and ski down the north face. However, four hours into their hike, snow has started to fall heavily. The closer they got to the peak, the heavier it fell. The group leader, Franz, has seemed worried. 'This is the first time I climbed in such bad conditions,' he has told the others in a worried voice. 'I didn't ski before in such thick snow. We should turn back.' But just as they have turned back, they realised that the path they have followed up the mountain was now buried under the snow! The other members of the group panicked. They would be stuck on the mountain until the snow cleared. To make matters worse, darkness was falling. 'I was in more dangerous situations than this,' Franz thought to himself. 'I can get us back safe and sound'. Just then the sound of an engine could be heard in the distance. It was a rescue helicopter. Luckily, the inn-keeper, who sensed the group was in danger when they didn't return in time, had sent for help.

Use your English

A Read and complete the *Exam Task*.

For questions **1 – 10**, read the text below. Use the word given in capitals at the end of some of the lines to form a word that fits the gap **in the same line**.

The challenges of the mountains

If you have ever visited mountains like the Himalayas in Tibet or the **(1)** _____ Alps, you will no doubt have experienced a range of emotions, from sheer **(2)** _____ to curiosity about what these breathtaking natural features have witnessed throughout the ages.

SWITZERLAND
AMAZE

People from all walks of life and from different **(3)** _____ have been visiting these places for centuries. **(4)** _____ groups of mountaineers from many countries have attempted to conquer the most difficult peaks in these mountain ranges. They start off full of **(5)** _____ to discover the secrets of the mountains. They also have the **(6)** _____ that they will be able to reach the peak without any unfortunate **(7)** _____. However, the truth is that even the most **(8)** _____ climbers experience moments where they think that nothing will go according to plan.

CIVILISE
NATION
EAGER
CONFIDE
OCCUR
PROFESSION

This can cause great **(9)** _____ and rather than feeling ecstatic about being in such wonderful surroundings, feelings of **(10)** _____ and defeat can creep up on them.

ANXIOUS
LONELY

B For questions 1 – 12, read the text below and think of the word which best fits each gap. Use only one word in each gap.

Safety and the city

What are the factors that help us decide whether a city **(1)** _____ a good place to live or not? It certainly should have all the modern amenities like schools, hospitals, banks and entertainment facilities that you'd expect to find in a large urban centre. But if you **(2)** _____ ever lived in a big city, you'll know that one of the most important factors is safety. Research into safety and fear in cities focuses **(3)** _____ factors such as how frequently accidents **(4)** _____ place as well as how high the crime rate is in order to rank them on the safe or dangerous scale. But even people who have **(5)** _____ been the victims of crime still have feelings of fear in the most 'dangerous' cities. If you find yourself **(6)** _____ a panic every time you're alone at a bus stop or when you **(7)** _____ walking down an empty city street at night, then maybe you need to move **(8)** _____ a safer city. In fact, people who **(9)** _____ to live in fear in their hometowns have often experienced great lifestyle changes simply by moving to a safer city. There's no point living in a bustling city if you fear for your life when you step outside. It's no surprise that Luxembourg, or Geneva and Zurich in Switzerland rate among **(10)** _____ safest cities in Europe. But given that many people associate Ireland with civil unrest, it is encouraging to hear that Dublin **(11)** _____ also been named one of Europe's safest cities for visitors and locals. This is because the Irish are thought to be among the least likely Europeans to get involved in violent crimes. So, if you are **(12)** _____ about moving city, give serious consideration to Dublin.

Writing: an opinion essay

A Read the writing task below and write **T** (true) or **F** (false).

You have seen this announcement in an international magazine for young people.

> **What benefits does your country have to offer visitors?**
> We will publish the most interesting articles next month.

Write your **article** in 140–190 words in an appropriate style.

1 You have to write an essay. ☐
2 You should write in a formal style. ☐
3 Your essay should have a title. ☐
4 You should compare your country to other countries. ☐
5 You should discuss why your country is the best place in the world to visit. ☐
6 You should only write about the advantages of visiting your country. ☐
7 You should write at least 190 words. ☐
8 Your essay should be organised into paragraphs. ☐

Learning Reminder

Organising your essay

- When writing an essay, don't forget to organise your ideas into paragraphs and to start each paragraph with a topic sentence. Your topic sentence should be clear and summarise the main idea of the paragraph so that the reader knows what the paragraph will be about.
- Start your essay with a good introduction, using expressions like *In my view ...* or *To my mind ...*
- Don't forget to summarise your essay in the conclusion, using expressions like *To sum up ...* or *In conclusion ...*

B Read the model essay and complete it with the topic sentences below.

a But what if you're a culture vulture?
b Whether you want to chill out or get a taste of the local culture, Spain has it all.
c So, you like nothing better than to soak up the sun on holiday.
d What do you look for when travelling abroad: sunny beaches or historical sites in bustling cities?

Spain: a destination for all tastes

(1) _____ Without a doubt, Spain is a destination that caters for a variety of tastes.

(2) _____ What are the top Spanish resorts? Try the Costa del Sol or an exotic island like Mallorca. The beautiful sunny beaches, golden sands and crystal clear waters won't fail to please. If you also crave clubbing, the nightlife there is unbeatable.

(3) _____ Spain boasts many exceptional historical sites like the Sagrada Familia church and other amazing buildings by Gaudi in Barcelona, Spain's most exciting city. If art is more your cup of tea, don't miss the Prado Museum in Madrid. Why not end a day of culture in one of Madrid's many tapas bars sampling local delicacies?

(4) _____ That's why it will remain a popular tourist destination for decades to come.

C Read and complete the *Exam Task* below. Don't forget to use the *Useful Expressions* on page 27 of your Student's Book.

Exam Task

You have seen this announcement in an international magazine for young people.

> **In what ways does travel broaden your horizons?**
> We will publish the most interesting articles next month.

Write your **essay** in 140–190 words in an appropriate style.

↻ Writing Reference p. 185 in Student's Book

Vocabulary

A Choose the correct answers.

1 I was in ___ after falling down a flight of stairs.

- a shame
- b misery
- c agony
- d anxietya

2 You'd better not play a ___ on Mr Higgins! He's got no sense of humour.

- a joke
- b role
- c reputation
- d joy

3 I think that multinational ___ have too much power.

- a customs
- b corporations
- c societies
- d cultures

4 Put the light on! I'm ___ of the dark!

- a terrified
- b frightful
- c disgusted
- d terrible

5 How can you possibly concentrate ___ your homework with the TV on?

- a to
- b for
- c in
- d on

6 When times are tough, people ___ to other countries.

- a trade
- b migrate
- c depart
- d spread

7 Who was ___ for building the Egyptian pyramids?

- a responsible
- b astonished
- c uncontrollable
- d anxious

8 My gap year was an amazing ___.

- a concept
- b effect
- c experience
- d phenomenon

9 Are storms a common ___ in your country?

- a occurrence
- b aspect
- c influence
- d event

10 We ___ business all over the world.

- a make
- b build
- c do
- d provide

11 Economics is difficult. It's all ___ to me!

- a French
- b Chinese
- c Greek
- d Swedish

12 Jan has saved so much ___ since she sold her car.

- a space
- b money
- c business
- d roadway

13 What's the matter? Don't ___.

- a cheer it up
- b focus on it
- c bottle it up
- d calm it down

14 There's no explanation for his ___ behaviour.

- a special
- b optimistic
- c severe
- d irrational

15 I was out of my ___ with worry when he was late.

- a seat
- b curiosity
- c skin
- d mind

16 I don't believe it. It's just Chinese ___.

- a tea
- b whispers
- c pandas
- d chiefs

17 I always buy from ___ producers to support the economy in my area.

- a local
- b international
- c universal
- d global

18 The two business partners are no longer on ___ terms.

- a specific
- b strict
- c good
- d desperate

19 We're doing a survey ___ on international trading.

- a based
- b responded
- c interested
- d connected

20 To my ___, I won a holiday to Sweden!

- a annoyance
- b eagerness
- c amazement
- d disgust

21 The audience ___ into applause at the end.

- a snapped
- b banged
- c burst
- d popped

22 Calm down! There's no need to ___ out.

- a run
- b freak
- c crash
- d flash

23 Why don't you come ___ with us to the park?

- a under
- b along
- c for
- d round

24 Did you fall ___ with your best friend again?

- a over
- b for
- c out
- d in

25 We were on the ___ of our seats all through the film.

- a edge
- b side
- c corner
- d top

26 It will ___ you good to go on holiday.

- a do
- b make
- c give
- d be

27 You shouldn't ___ up your feelings.

- a box
- b carton
- c pack
- d bottle

28 It took him years to get ___ the loss of his mother.

- a out
- b over
- c off
- d on

Grammar

B **Choose the correct answers.**

1 Rory ___ to Spain since 1990.
- **a** isn't
- **c** hasn't been
- **b** wasn't
- **d** wasn't being

2 Lisa ___ to get very anxious at exam time.
- **a** use
- **c** has used
- **b** used
- **d** would

3 Why do you ___ your new teacher so much?
- **a** disliked
- **c** dislike
- **b** disliking
- **d** to dislike

4 She ___ that book on world geography for weeks.
- **a** reads
- **c** has read
- **b** is reading
- **d** has been reading

5 I haven't booked my flights ___.
- **a** yet
- **c** already
- **b** still
- **d** just

6 The plane landed, taxied along the runway and then ___ to a standstill.
- **a** has come
- **c** was coming
- **b** came
- **d** did come

7 I always ___ sad at the end of term.
- **a** feel
- **c** was feeling
- **b** am feeling
- **d** have felt

8 Why ___ earlier?
- **a** Tom was crying
- **c** was Tom crying
- **b** has Tom cried
- **d** has Tom been crying

9 My boss ___ a meeting in Strasbourg at the moment.
- **a** is attending
- **c** has attended
- **b** attends
- **d** has been attending

10 We haven't been ___ goods to Europe for long.
- **a** export
- **c** exported
- **b** exporting
- **d** exports

11 Mum ___ shopping in London every summer.
- **a** used to
- **c** would go
- **b** have gone
- **d** are going

12 What time ___ arrive?
- **a** has Mike's train
- **c** Mike's train
- **b** was Mike's train
- **d** does Mike's train

13 In Amsterdam, I ___ a bike wherever I want to go.
- **a** ride
- **c** have ridden
- **b** am riding
- **d** rode

14 Does Hugh ___ reading about ancient civilisations?
- **a** enjoys
- **c** enjoyed
- **b** enjoying
- **d** enjoy

15 They ___ out of the safari at the last minute.
- **a** were chickening
- **c** chickened
- **b** have been chickening
- **d** chicken

16 We ___ to Malta next week.
- **a** are going
- **c** going
- **b** go
- **d** have gone

17 How many times ___ this film?
- **a** have you seen
- **c** do you see
- **b** did you see
- **d** have you been seeing

18 This is the worst CD I ___!
- **a** ever hear
- **c** have ever heard
- **b** ever hearing
- **d** have ever been hearing

19 While Dan was sleeping, Ann ___ a magazine.
- **a** read
- **c** reads
- **b** was reading
- **d** has read

20 I ___ my passport at the airport last week.
- **a** lose
- **c** have lost
- **b** lost
- **d** did lose

21 Did we ___ go to the same nursery school?
- **a** would
- **c** use to
- **b** used to
- **d** using to

22 Those jeans ___ too much money!
- **a** are costing
- **c** is costing
- **b** costs
- **d** cost

23 'Where's your cousin?' 'She ___ in Australia at the moment.'
- **a** studies
- **c** study
- **b** is studying
- **d** is study

24 I ___ your ridiculous story.
- **a** don't believe
- **c** 'm not believing
- **b** not believe
- **d** don't believing

25 Who's been ___ my cheese?
- **a** ate
- **c** eating
- **b** eaten
- **d** eat

26 They ___ living in the big city.
- **a** were loving
- **c** loved
- **b** are loving
- **d** to love

27 'I'm exhausted.' '___ you been working all afternoon?'
- **a** Are
- **c** Did
- **b** Do
- **d** Have

28 We ___ swimming for ages.
- **a** didn't be
- **c** haven't
- **b** weren't
- **d** haven't been

Reading

A Read the *Exam Reminder*. What should you do first?

_____

B Now complete the *Exam Task*.

The life of Joyce Carol Vincent: A tragic tale of popularity to obscurity to fame

Scriptwriter and director Carol Morley's latest film *Dreams of a Life*, a nominee for the Grierson Award for best documentary at the 2011 London Film Festival, tells a difficult tale. **1** ☐ As a result of the film, the attractive Witney Houston lookalike is sure to achieve celebrity status, if not to become a legend.

On 25ᵗʰ January 2006, council officials arrived at a dingy one-roomed flat in Wood Green, London. **2** ☐ On entering the flat, they were met with a disturbing sight: a decomposed skeleton was lying on the couch with the television still on. Forensic tests showed that the skeleton was of a woman in her late thirties who had died almost three years earlier; dental records and an old holiday photo helped to identify the woman as Joyce Carol Vincent. The cause of her death, however, still remains a mystery.

On hearing the story of the unfortunate woman, director Carol Morley was intrigued to find out more about who she was. She was fascinated by how someone could die in this way and for nobody to notice she was missing. **3** ☐ During her investigation, she managed to track down several of Joyce's former friends, colleagues and boyfriends. They all reacted with disbelief on hearing about Joyce's fate. They all described her as a very popular, outgoing person who had always been surrounded by other people. A few years before her death, she had been climbing up the career ladder in her high-paying job at a reputable accounting firm. **4** ☐ Neither could they imagine that the fun-loving Joyce they once knew had been so alone during her last days that her absence hadn't been noticed by anyone.

The more Morley found out about Joyce, the more she was convinced that she had to make a film about her life. **5** ☐ In the 1980s, she was friends with a musician called Kirk Thorne who used to record punk sensation Captain Sensible in his recording studio. In this same studio, he had also recorded Joyce who dreamt of becoming a singer one day. In her youth, Joyce had also dated a baronet, an MP and Alistair Abrahams, the former tour manager of a famous soul singer. Together, they even shook hands with Nelson Mandela at a concert given in his honour, and Joyce appears on the broadcasted version of the concert watched by millions in 60 countries. Clearly, she had been a woman with good connections.

Morley's documentary plays tribute to this extraordinary woman and her tragic story. **6** ☐ The film brings home to us how being indifferent to those around us – friends, relatives, neighbours or just passers-by – can lead to exceptionally sad circumstances. Having said that, Morley's point is not to depress her audience, but to set alarm bells ringing. Now, more than ever, we need to nurture our relationships; we need to re-establish the concept of community spirit and keep Joyce's memory alive.

Six sentences have been removed from the text. Choose from the sentences **A – G** the one which fits each gap (**1 – 6**). There is one extra sentence which you do not need to use.

A It is also a wake-up call for those who watch it.

B None of her former colleagues could understand how she ended up living in such poor conditions.

C The tenant hadn't paid any rent for three years, so the local council had decided to evict her and take possession of the property again.

D But Morley wasn't the only one interested in making Joyce's life into a film.

E It seemed that Joyce hadn't only been popular with the friends Morley had managed to find, but also with several celebrities.

F It focuses on the life and death of Joyce Carol Vincent.

G This curiosity was the spark that initiated a long investigation by Morley into Joyce's life.

Vocabulary

A **The words in bold are in the wrong sentences. Write each word next to the correct sentence.**

1 There's a **gossip** going round that the singer is pregnant! _____
2 Who is your favourite TV **character**? _____
3 I love reading celebrity **shame** on the Internet. _____
4 Sia's biggest **account** is coming second in a talent contest. _____
5 What a **disgrace** you can't come to the film premiere! _____
6 Do you have a Twitter or Facebook **personality**? _____
7 Mickey Mouse is still a popular cartoon **accomplishment**. _____
8 It's an absolute **rumour** that celebrities are paid huge sums of money just to appear in public. _____

B **Complete the sentences with the correct form of the words.**

1 To our _____, the charity ball was cancelled.   **ASTONISH**
2 The Prince's press _____ said he was much better after his illness.   **REPRESENT**
3 Would you like to be rich and famous and have lots of _____?   **SERVE**
4 The young musician is an _____ to us all.   **INSPIRE**
5 The film was shot on _____ in Miami.   **LOCATE**
6 Stars can't expect to have fame and _____!   **PRIVATE**
7 The royal wedding received a lot of _____.   **PUBLIC**
8 Stella McCartney makes _____ designer clothes.   **STYLE**

C **Complete the text with these words.**

break   figure   influential   money   notorious   qualified   reputation   scandal

When Doctor Conrad Murray left the University of Arizona as a (**1**) _____ cardiologist, little did he know what lay in store for him career-wise. After years of building up a (**2**) _____ as a doctor with a heart, as he often treated patients without health insurance free of charge, Murray got a lucky (**3**) _____. He was offered a job that would make most doctors green with envy – as Michael Jackson's full-time personal doctor. The pop star, who was (**4**) _____ for his health problems and who was made of (**5**) _____, even paid him an astounding $150,000 per month for the position! On July 29th 2010, the day that the star died in his home, Murray had been on duty. Although he was freed of any blame for the star's death at first, Jackson's (**6**) _____ family were convinced that someone had murdered the star. It didn't take long for Murray to be put at the centre of the (**7**) _____ and for him to be put on trial for manslaughter. However, during the trial he became a popular (**8**) _____ with the media and gained celebrity status himself with fans all over the world pledging their support for him. He was, however, found guilty of manslaughter.

Grammar

Past Perfect Simple & Past Perfect Continuous

A Find and correct the mistakes in the sentences.

1 They had stayed at their beach house when the fire broke out. _____
2 How many films had he been starring in before making his latest one? _____
3 She had watched the news when the kids came home. _____
4 The agent had been representing hundreds of singers in her career. _____
5 He had never been visiting Hollywood until last spring. _____
6 The star had walked along the red carpet when she tripped and fell. _____

B Complete the sentences with the Past Perfect Simple or the Past Perfect Continuous form of the verbs in brackets.

1 Princess Diana _____ (stay) in Paris when she died.
2 Lady Gaga _____ (get) ready for the show when her heel snapped.
3 Boy George _____ (not be) in prison before.
4 The actor _____ (never play) such a difficult role.
5 _____ the journalist _____ (nose about) for information when he was thrown out of the hotel?
6 I _____ (not ask) for an autograph, but the footballer gave me one anyway.

C Complete the text by writing one word in each gap.

At the end of October 2011, celebrity Kim Kardashian made an important announcement. She (1) _____ just filed for divorce from her husband, Kris Humphries. The couple, who had (2) _____ dating for only six months when Humphries popped the question, (3) _____ tied the knot only 72 days earlier. Gossip columnists (4) _____ among the first to realise that all (5) _____ not well in the Kardashian-Humphries house. Rumours started flying when Kim, who had (6) _____ taken her vows 'till death do them part', started attending social engagements on her own. 'Had their relationship (7) _____ ended?' was the big question on everybody's lips. The answer didn't take long in coming. Yes, it (8) _____!

Listening

A Read the *Exam Reminder*. What should you do the first time you listen?

_____

B ▣▶▎▎ Listen and complete the *Exam Task*.

Exam Reminder

Identifying synonyms
- Remember to think of other ways of saying the key words in the statements.
- Don't forget to try to summarise the main point each speaker makes when you listen the first time, and take notes.
- Then compare your notes with the statements to find the best match.

Exam Task

You will hear five people talking about their favourite celebrities. For questions **1 – 5**, choose from the list **A – H** what each person says about them. Use the letters only once. There are three extra letters which you do not need to use.

1 Speaker 1 ☐
2 Speaker 2 ☐
3 Speaker 3 ☐
4 Speaker 4 ☐
5 Speaker 5 ☐

A He's not afraid to take risks.
B I am totally obsessed with this celebrity.
C I admire him for things he does other than his paid work.
D His most recent work didn't live up to his usual standards.
E He's the highest paid celebrity on Earth.
F Although he's not a comedian, he really makes me laugh.
G She was so funny when I met her.
H I actually used to know her at school.

C ▣▶▎▎ Listen again and check your answers.

Grammar

Past Simple vs Past Perfect (Simple & Continuous)

A Complete the sentences with the Past Simple or the Past Perfect Simple or Continuous form of these verbs.

act be change end go have join never belong offer play walk write

1 We _____ the time of our lives when Matt Dillon _____ into the club.
2 _____ Bruce Willis _____ for long when they _____ him a role in *Moonlighting*?
3 U2 _____ for over two hours when the concert _____.
4 She _____ to any other band when she _____ the Bangles.
5 Before he _____ on stage, he _____ a new song.
6 Somebody _____ the guest list and my name _____ no longer on it.

B Complete the second sentences so that they have a similar meaning to the first sentences using the words in bold. Use between two and five words.

1 It was the first time I had met a celebrity.
   never
   I _____ a celebrity before.
2 Before giving me her autograph, she shook my hand.
   once
   She gave me her autograph _____ my hand.
3 Seeing her favourite star in the flesh made her ecstatic.
   because
   She was ecstatic _____ her favourite star in the flesh.

4 In 2005, Cary played his first international match.
   had
   Cary _____ an international match before 2005.
5 At the time of her death, Amy Winehouse was twenty-seven years old.
   she
   When _____, Amy Winehouse was twenty-seven.
6 After a two-year world tour, the band needed a break.
   touring
   The band _____ two years, so they needed a break.

Use your English

A Read the *Exam Reminder* and complete the *Exam Task*.

Exam Task

For questions **1 – 12**, read the text below and think of the word which best fits each gap. Use only **one** word in each gap.

Robert Burns

Robert Burns, Scotland's greatest poet, was born in 1759. (1) _____ an early age he had to help his father on his farm, as (2) _____ as attend school lessons.

When he was 22, he moved to Irvine, where he began to learn about making cloth. Shortly after (3) _____ arrival, the factory in which he was training was destroyed by fire, so he started a farm with his younger brother Gilbert.

While he was living on the farm, he concentrated (4) _____ writing poems and fell (5) _____ a local girl, Jean Armour. Robert wanted to marry her, but her father (6) _____ not allow him to do so. This took Robert (7) _____ surprise, and since he could not (8) _____ used to the idea of being unable to marry her, he decided to leave the country. (9) _____ very little money, Robert had to obtain the fare for the voyage by selling some poems. Just as he was about to leave, he (10) _____ advised to publish some of the poems he (11) _____ written. He received a large sum of money for the poetry and was then (12) _____ to get married to Jean.

B For questions 1–10, read the text below and decide which answer (a, b, c or d) best fits each gap.

A new breed of superstar

Nowadays, many people become household names through professions that were once thought of as simply respectable, rather than glamorous. Take lawyers, for example. Getting a job with a top law (1) ___ may not only ensure financial security due to the astronomical (2) ___ lawyers can command, but it may also bring the same superstar (3) ___ as that of a Hollywood actor. There are very few Americans who do not (4) ___ the name of the independent public prosecutor, Kenneth Starr. But a person must be (5) ___ out to be a lawyer in order to be successful. Firstly, a persuasive character is essential to getting every member of the jury to (6) ___ in with your line of argument. Secondly, the (7) ___ to judge character is vital, since a witness's (8) ___ to a question may be more significant than the answer given. (9) ___ , leadership qualities are fundamental. Top lawyers do not have the time to (10) ___ all the research necessary in a case by themselves. As a result, they have to set an example for those under their command, so that they can count on the team to work conscientiously.

1	a company	b firm	c industry	d business
2	a tips	b fares	c rewards	d fees
3	a level	b fame	c status	d stance
4	a recognise	b remind	c memorise	d retain
5	a suited	b cut	c stood	d made
6	a go	b call	c get	d fall
7	a certainty	b capability	c will	d ability
8	a look	b reaction	c action	d response
9	a Eventually	b Finally	c Ultimately	d Conclusively
10	a take	b do	c make	d carry

C For questions 1 – 8, complete the second sentence so that it has a similar meaning to the first sentence, using the word given. Do not change the word given. You must use between two and five words, including the word given.

1 She may have been rich and famous, but she didn't think she was better than others.

   down

   She _____ others even though she was rich and famous.

2 I started living in Paris in 2003, but Mark didn't move here until 2008.

   for

   I _____ five years in Paris when Mark moved here.

3 Why don't we go to see a film later?

   shall

   _____ to see a film later?

4 It's so annoying how he talks about the famous people he knows all the time.

   name

   I wish he _____ all the time.

5 The singer suddenly fired her agent without any explanation.

   out

   She fired her agent _____ .

6 2013 will be my tenth year in show business.

   have

   I _____ in show business for ten years by 2013.

7 When we got to the stadium, the concert was finished.

   by

   The concert _____ the time we got to the stadium.

8 The actors from the film hated each other and fought a lot.

   tension

   There was _____ on the film set.

Writing: a story(1)

Learning Reminder

Thinking about the details
- Remember to keep your storyline simple and to include details about the place, the time, the characters and the action.
- It's important for the reader to be able to follow the sequence of events, so use narrative tenses and time phrases.
- Try to use a variety of structures to make your story more vivid. For example, using direct speech brings your story alive.
- Always be careful with punctuation and spelling.

A Read the writing task below and answer the questions.

You have decided to enter an international short story competition. The competition rules say that the story must begin with the words:

It was a dream come true for Celia.

Write your **story** in 140–190 words in an appropriate style.

1 Do you have to begin or end your story with the words given?
2 Who will the main character be?
3 Will the story focus on something positive or negative?
4 Will the story take place in the past, present or future?

B Read the model story and circle the correct words.

It was a dream come true for Celia. The big day (**1**) was arriving / had arrived at last. She couldn't believe she was finally going to see her favourite rock star, Ricky Rotten in the flesh.

She was (**2**) ecstatic / glad as she walked to the concert hall, while listening to her favourite Ricky tracks on her MP3. Out of the (**3**) blue / warning, someone violently pushed past her and yanked her bag from her shoulder. Celia panicked. Her ticket was in that bag. She wouldn't be able to get into the concert after all!

Heartbroken, Celia (**4**) slumped / went down on the step of a nearby shop and began to sob (**5**) sadly / uncontrollably. Just then a limousine drove up beside her. Slowly, the window rolled down and a familiar face (**6**) was appearing / appeared. 'Why all the tears?' (**7**) said / asked the man in the passenger's seat. Celia looked up in disbelief: it was Ricky Rotten!

After she explained the whole story, Ricky suggested going to the concert and the backstage party together. Celia pinched herself to see if she was dreaming. Entering the concert hall, she felt like she (**8**) had floated / was floating on air.

C Read and complete the *Exam Task* below. Don't forget to use the *Useful Expressions* on page 41 of your Student's Book.

Exam Task

You have decided to enter an international short story competition. The competition rules say that the story must begin with the words:

Darren was sure it would be a night to remember.

Write your story in 140–190 words in an appropriate style.

↻ Writing Reference p. 181 in Student's Book

Reading

A Read the *Exam Reminder*. What should you do to get the main ideas?

_____

B Now complete the *Exam Task*.

Sherford: A green city of the future

A Ranked amongst the top five green cities of the future, Sherford in England has got to be one of the most exciting urban projects of the 21st century. With construction due to commence in 2014, the thinking behind the new town is to provide a solution to urban sprawl slum areas and the ecological problems that come with them. In other words, it will be a shining example of sustainable urbanism.

The proposed location for the new town is in one of the greenest parts of the English countryside: Devon. Although it will be a modern town with all the necessary facilities for modern-day living, the town will have a traditional feel to it. Local architectural designs will be used to make sure the town has a distinctive Devon character. Developers, Red Tree, claim that their aim is for Sherford to take 'the best from the past and move it forward'. They have a vision of a town where social, economic and environmental sustainability will prosper.

B But just how will they achieve this? Sustainable towns and cities must meet the strictest criteria. In order to be socially sustainable, they must be organised into self-contained neighbourhoods which combine living, working and shopping. Sherford, which will be organised into four neighbourhoods, will take this one step further. All its communities will be accessible to people from all income bracket and all ethnic groups. A wide range of homes will be available for rent or purchase, with the cheaper homes being built alongside the most expensive ones to avoid any discrimination that may arise. However, it won't be obvious just by looking at the homes which ones are the most affordable ones. By avoiding creating rich neighbourhoods and poor neighbourhoods, it is hoped that residents will feel a greater sense of equality.

In terms of economic sustainability, eco towns must be able to support the livelihoods of the local residents. For the first time in a century, a British town will be built along a high street with a lively market. As a market town, Sherford promises to be a bustling commercial centre with shops, local businesses and services. This will ensure that people who live locally, can work and earn their living locally. As a result, the town will be financially sustainable.

C Most importantly of all, however, Sherford – like all eco towns – will be environmentally sustainable. Green cities must reduce or eliminate the use of fossil fuels, adopt sustainable building practices, create green spaces and ensure good air quality. It is hoped that this attractive town will discourage people from writing graffiti on the buildings and so not allowing the gritty side of a town to emerge. It will also be a safe place for people to live. One of the developers commented, 'No one will get mugged in Sherford.' Sherford will be a walkable city. Local schools, shops, parks and other facilities will be within walking distances of housing. There will also be an energy-efficient transport system that residents will be encouraged to use to travel within the town and cars will be banned from parts of the town centre. But one of the biggest bonuses for all future residents is that they will be provided with their own free bicycle so that they will have another alternative to private cars for getting from A to B. Furthermore, 50% of the town's energy will be supplied using clean, renewable sources such as solar and wind power. 170 acres of woodland and 500 acres of parkland will also help to improve the quality of air in the town and surrounding area. They will also create recreational areas for residents and be home to local species of plants and animals.

D So when can you move in? If all goes according to plan, building will begin on Sherford in 2014. During the first phase, 2,750 homes will be constructed within five years. The completed project, which will include 5,500 homes divided between the four neighbourhoods and the town centre, will take between 12-15 years to complete. For the majority of the locals, it will have been a long time in coming, but well worth waiting for.

Exam Task

You are going to read an article about a new town. For questions **1 – 10**, choose the paragraphs (**A – D**). The paragraphs may be chosen more than once.

Which paragraph says

1 the proposed location for the new town is Devon? ☐
2 building will begin in 2014? ☐
3 cheaper homes will be built alongside more expensive ones? ☐
4 local architectural designs will be used to keep the Devon character? ☐
5 facilities in the town will be within walking distance of housing? ☐
6 future residents will be provided with their own free bicycle? ☐
7 50% of the town's energy will be supplied by renewable sources? ☐
8 Sherford will be organised into four neighbourhoods? ☐
9 it will take 12–15 years to complete? ☐
10 people will live locally and can work and earn their living locally? ☐

Vocabulary

A Complete the words in the sentences.

1 Slow down a bit; you're approaching a s _ _ _ _ b _ _ _!

2 I prefer to live in the inner city than on the o _ _ _ _ _ _ _ _.

3 The l _ _ _ _ _ _ _ has kindly agreed to reduce our rent.

4 Some people love cities, but I think they're c _ _ _ _ _ _ _ j _ _ _ _ _ _.

5 The two politicians lived together as f _ _ _ _ _ _ _ _ when they were at university.

6 Knightsbridge is one of the most expensive d _ _ _ _ _ _ _ _ in London.

B Choose the correct answers.

1 Our new ___ pays us £400 a month rent.
   a inhabitant   b tenant   c resident

2 You can't drive here; it's a(n) ___
   a avenue   b zebra crossing   c pedestrian area

3 What does that ___ say?
   a street sign   b speed camera   c town hall

4 Many shops have had to close in the city's main ___ district.
   a traffic   b outskirts   c commercial

5 Jan wants to get out of her ___ city and head for the countryside.
   a resident   b industrial   c factory

6 Let's have a ___ on the town; it's been ages since we had fun!
   a night   b walk   c talk

7 ___ pollution is one of the biggest problems in large cities.
   a Noise   b Surrounding   c Seasonal

8 Five ___ were arrested yesterday for illegal occupation of a villa.
   a flatmates   b landlords   c squatters

C Complete the text by writing one word in each gap.

Jump on the Bandra wagon!

If you're anxious to get (1) _____ for a while, and want to sample a bit of Asian promise, head for Bandra. For many, it's the hippest suburb in India's most populous city, Mumbai, and offers visitors and locals an exciting mix of old and new. Portuguese architecture blends well with the spacious, trendy residences that many Bollywood stars have moved (2) _____ in recent years. In comparison to most locals, these stars (3) _____ luxurious lives and can often be seen hanging (4) _____ in the suburb's many up-market restaurants and bars. If you want to (5) _____ the town red alongside these local celebrities, book a table at Hakkasan restaurant, for a night to remember. There are also many less expensive restaurants if your wallet can't handle the prices paid by the stars. Bandra is crammed with good, cheap restaurants that cater for people from all (6) _____ of life. You can even sample *chaat* and *pani puri*, Indian delicacies sold by the many roadside street vendors. From Mumbai, you can get to Bandra easily by train – be warned, though, trains tend to be overcrowded. If you value personal (7) _____, however, opt for a taxi and marvel at the view of Mumbai's skyline during the ride.

City Living **4** 25

Grammar

Future Forms

A Find and correct the mistakes in the sentences.

1 Shall we be going into town for pizza tonight? _____
2 By this time tomorrow, Sharon will leave Paris. _____
3 I promise I will be coming to visit you more often when you move to your new house. _____
4 The company has just decided they will be creating a roof garden. _____
5 Call me as soon as you will arrive in Sydney. _____
6 In a week's time, residents will use the new road. _____

B Complete the sentences with the correct future form of the verbs in brackets.

1 Building work on the new skyscraper _____ (finish) by this time next month.
2 Jack promises he _____ (not run) for election at the town council again.
3 _____ I _____ (give) you a lift to the train station in the morning?
4 Watch out! You _____ (crash into) that street sign!
5 I've made up my mind. I _____ (paint) the town red tonight.
6 This time next year, we _____ (live) in Boringville for 15 years.
7 Do experts think that life in big cities _____ (improve) in the future?
8 _____ you _____ (help) me take care of the roof garden?

Listening

A Read the *Exam Reminder*. What must you always do?

_____

B `4.1` ▶ **Listen and complete the *Exam Task*.**

Exam Reminder

Preparing to listen

- Remember to read all the questions first and make sure you understand them.
- Make notes while you listen and if you get stuck on a question, don't waste time, move onto the next one.
- When you get to the end, don't forget to go back and complete any missing answers.
- Remember you must always answer every question.

Exam Task

You will hear a radio interview about nicknames given to cities. For questions **1 – 6**, choose the best answer (**a, b** or **c**).

1 What does Vanessa not like doing on holiday?
   a mixing with other celebrities
   b visiting local places of interest
   c going to the beach

2 Why does Vanessa travel by public transport in foreign cities?
   a She can't afford a limousine.
   b It's the easiest way to get about.
   c so that she can get to know the city and its people better

3 Vanessa's book is about
   a cities in the USA.
   b cities which have nicknames.
   c Los Angeles and New York only.

4 Where did Vanessa get the idea for her book?
   a from her diary of the cities she has been to
   b from another guide book
   c from a trip she made to Paris

5 What does Vanessa say Paris and Edinburgh have in common?
   a They have the same nickname.
   b They have impressive historic buildings on hills in the city centres.
   c They were both significant places for scholars in the past.

6 What makes San Francisco special for Vanessa?
   a the Golden Gate Bridge
   b its large population
   c its atmosphere

C `4.1` ▶ **Listen again and check your answers.**

Grammar

Countable & Uncountable Nouns

A Underline the countable nouns and circle the uncountable nouns in the sentences.

1 We've got too much furniture so we're selling this table.
2 They sell fantastic jewellery, but I only bought a brooch.
3 Yuck! This chair is covered in hair!
4 The firefighter warned the school children not to play with fire.
5 He wasn't given the job as he didn't have relevant experience.
6 Put all the broken glass in the bin, please.
7 Would you like milk on your cereal?
8 I usually love chocolate, but these caramel-filled chocolates are disgusting!

B Circle the correct words.

1 Many / Much residents feel the council must provide better amenities.
2 There are a lots of / lot of criminals in big cities.
3 Would you like some / any coffee?
4 There is no / any room to build new houses here.
5 Lots of / No people prefer urban to rural areas.
6 Is there much paper / papers in the printer?
7 Would you like a bar / slice of cheese in your sandwich?
8 How many travels / trips have you been on this year?
9 Is / Are physics a difficult subject?
10 Local politics was / were not something I wanted to get involved in.

Use your English

A For questions 1 – 10, read the text below and think of the word which best fits each gap. Use only one word in each gap.

The City that Never Sleeps

With a population of over 8 million spread over 790 km², New York City has (1) _____ residents per square kilometre than any other city in the US. The five boroughs that make up the city, Manhattan, Queens, The Bronx, Brooklyn and Staten Island joined to become one city (2) _____ 1898. But New York (3) _____ not always the name given to this part of the US. The first people to settle these lands were Dutch colonists. In 1624, they set up a trading post here and gave it the name New Amsterdam. The name changed, however, in 1664 (4) _____ the English king took control of the lands and gave them to his brother the Duke of York as a gift. This led (5) _____ its name being changed in honour of the Duke. The name New York has been used ever (6) _____. The Statue of Liberty, (7) _____ is one of the many symbols of the city, arrived towards the end of the 19th and beginning of the 20th century. But long before the Statue of Liberty arrived, the city (8) _____ enjoyed a long history. Today the city is the biggest city in the US, but it also (9) _____ to be the capital. For five short years from 1785-1790, New Yorkers (10) _____ inhabitants of the country's centre of administration. Nowadays, it is a popular tourist destination and every year thousands of people from all over the world flock to the City that Never Sleeps to visit famous places like Times Square, Broadway theatres and Central Park. Whatever they come here to see, they aren't disappointed. One thing is for sure, New York will continue to be a major attraction for many years to come.

B Read the *Exam Reminder*. What is the last step you should remember to do for each question?

_____

C Now complete the *Exam Task*.

Exam Task

For questions **1 – 10**, read the text below and decide which answer (**a, b, c** or **d**) best fits the gap.

Smartcards – a sustainable solution to urban mobility

City-dwellers are constantly on the move. Whether they are going for a **(1)** ___ on the town, getting to work, or taking the kids to school, **(2)** ___ of large cities never seem to stop. As they **(3)** ___ such busy lives, creating sustainable transport systems is becoming more and more important. Use of private cars may seem like the ideal way to get from A to B, but cities soon become congested as a result. In the long run, the more cars on the road, the longer it takes to get from one **(4)** ___ to another. In order to promote mobility and to reduce **(5)** ___ pollution in cities, an effective transport grid must be in place. Buses, trams and trains are the most common way of travelling in cities, but it can get really frustrating when passengers need to use more of these means in the course of one **(6)** ___. Citizens of many European cities have been **(7)** ___ with the Smartcard ticketing system which has been introduced to deal with this problem. In London, for example, the Oyster card is now used on 80% of all journeys on public transport. **(8)** ___ a doubt it is much more popular than old-fashioned paper tickets. All the user has to do is keep the card topped up and all the stress and **(9)** ___ of queuing up for tickets for each leg of their journey is gone. The success of the card has **(10)** ___ the expectations of passengers and transport providers with 34 million Oyster cards having been sold between 2003 and 2010. It is certain to catch on in other major cities worldwide in response to the increasing need to transform concrete jungles into liveable urban centres.

1	**a** talk	**b** night	**c** break	**d** life
2	**a** lodgers	**b** flatmates	**c** residents	**d** squatters
3	**a** lead	**b** settle	**c** move	**d** deal
4	**a** alley	**b** space	**c** location	**d** scene
5	**a** sound	**b** chatter	**c** seasonal	**d** noise
6	**a** voyage	**b** journey	**c** excursion	**d** expedition
7	**a** encouraged	**b** sponsored	**c** marked	**d** impressed
8	**a** Without	**b** Under	**c** In	**d** Behind
9	**a** shock	**b** tension	**c** rumours	**d** victory
10	**a** lived up to	**b** started out	**c** catered to	**d** come in for

Writing: an article

A Read the writing task below and tick the things you have to do.

You have seen this announcement in an international magazine for young people.

> **What will life be like in big cities in the twenty-second century? How can we stop them from becoming concrete jungles?**
>
> We will publish the most interesting articles next month.

Write your **article** in 140–190 words in an appropriate style.

1 include a title ☐
2 write about present-day cities ☐
3 concentrate on cities of the future ☐
4 discuss why people should live in cities in the next century ☐
5 make some suggestions about how cities of the future might be built ☐
6 write in a formal style ☐
7 use a variety of structures ☐

Learning Reminder

Engaging your reader

- Remember to use direct and indirect questions in order to engage the reader and encourage them to think about their own opinion concerning the topic of the article.
- Don't forget to use a variety of structures such as the passive voice, conditional sentences, comparisons, etc. to show that you have a range of language.
- Finally, once you have finished your article, check your spelling, punctuation and grammar.

B Read the example article and answer the questions.

Twenty-second century city life

More and more people are attracted by the bright city lights and life in the fast lane. But what will cities be like in the next century? Also, how can we prevent them turning into impersonal concrete jungles?

The population of big cities worldwide is predicted to increase dramatically over the next century. Have you ever wondered how this will affect urban life? For a start, more housing will be needed and amenities like schools and hospitals will have to cater for larger populations.

As you can imagine, the biggest challenge will be to make our cities liveable. Building suitable housing in the suburbs and providing quick and efficient transport systems into cities is one way to ensure inner cities don't become too crowded. Also, green roofs should be made compulsory on all city centre buildings. Just think of the benefits to the environment if concrete buildings become living, breathing constructions!

Twenty-second century cities are sure to be busy places. Let's hope they become bustling urban centres and not concrete jungles.

1 How has the writer tried to involve the reader?
2 What has the writer done immediately after the question in paragraph 2?
3 What suggestions has the writer included in the article?
4 Do you think these suggestions are suitable?

C Read and complete the *Exam Task* below. Don't forget to use the *Useful Expressions* on page 53 of your Student's Book.

Exam Task

You have seen this announcement in an international magazine for young people.

> **Will the public transport system in your country's capital be able to cater for increasing numbers of city dwellers? What changes might be necessary to cope with greater demand for public transport?**
>
> We will publish the most interesting articles next month.

Write your **article** in 140–190 words in an appropriate style.

➲ Writing Reference p. 182 in Student's Book

Vocabulary

A Choose the correct answers.

1 I'm looking for a new ___ to share the rent and bills.
- a squatter
- c flatmate
- b landlord
- d inhabitant

2 Kim seems to get involved in a new ___ every week!
- a scandal
- c gossip
- b disgrace
- d shame

3 The couple's marriage was just a ___ stunt.
- a privacy
- c publicity
- b reputation
- d personality

4 Inner ___ areas can be dangerous.
- a city
- c suburb
- b urban
- d district

5 The speed ___ in this part of town is 50 km.
- a bump
- c camera
- b sign
- d limit

6 Cars can't park in a(n) ___ area.
- a environmental
- c zebra
- b pedestrian
- d conventional

7 Chad made a ___ for himself on a reality show.
- a break
- c character
- b money
- d name

8 You look very ___. Have you been working out?
- a chubby
- c toned
- b regal
- d plain

9 The paparazzi are ___ to be waiting outside the house.
- a guaranteed
- c notorious
- b accomplished
- d qualified

10 Let's ___ the town red tonight!
- a deal
- c paint
- b lead
- d grab

11 Why didn't you stop? The ___ was red!
- a junction
- c pavement
- b parking meter
- d traffic light

12 I wish you wouldn't ___ drop all the time!
- a person
- c name
- b star
- d rumour

13 By all ___, this is the worst film she's starred in so far.
- a accounts
- c comments
- b scenes
- d prices

14 The city is ___ pressure to build more schools.
- a behind
- c in
- b under
- d by

15 Send your complaints to the mayor at the ___.
- a ghost town
- c concrete jungle
- b town hall
- d outskirts

16 Do you know what the population ___ of Cairo is?
- a race
- c density
- b space
- d lane

17 Now that he's a star, he treats us like ___!
- a agents
- c fans
- b servants
- d representatives

18 I don't have a Facebook ___.
- a service
- c account
- b accomplishment
- d hit

19 The residents of Villa Arriba ___ on the residents of Villa Abajo.
- a catch
- c come in
- b cater
- d look down

20 Only the ___ rich can live in this district.
- a filthy
- c classy
- b royal
- d dirty

21 It's a nice idea, but I don't think it will ___ on.
- a take
- c catch
- b have
- d bring

22 Why does he look ___ on people?
- a up
- c down
- b over
- d round

23 His latest novel ___ in for a lot of harsh criticism.
- a came
- c ran
- b went
- d fell

24 Greg has been ___ a lot of pressure.
- a on
- c under
- b at
- d over

25 The meeting was held ___ private.
- a to
- c under
- b on
- d in

26 Let's ___ somewhere for the weekend.
- a get away
- c get around
- b go along
- d go over

27 I didn't understand the point he was trying to get ___ to us.
- a in
- c across
- b on
- d at

28 We really ___ the town red last night!
- a painted
- c brushed
- b coloured
- d covered

Grammar

B Choose the correct answers.

1 They ___ down the Berlin Wall back in 1989.
  a had pulled   c had been pulling
  b pulled   d will pull

2 The actress was wearing extremely big ___.
  a glass   c luggage
  b hair   d trousers

3 You can't go to Switzerland without bringing me back a ___ of chocolate.
  a pair   c bar
  b jar   d carton

4 Watch out! That tram ___ crash into us!
  a will   c is going to
  b shall   d will have

5 This time next month, we ___ in Madrid for four years.
  a will live   c are going to live
  b will have been living d lived

6 There were ___ stars at the film premiere.
  a any   c lots
  b little   d few

7 Would you like another slice of ___?
  a pizza   c grapes
  b soup   d cereal

8 Was it the first time you ___ Brussels?
  a had been visiting   c shall visit
  b had visited   d will have visited

9 ___ arrange for front row seats for tomorrow's play?
  a Will I   c Shall I
  b Had I   d Am I going to

10 The book gives many ___ about what to see in Goa.
  a advice   c experience
  b tips   d permission

11 That's a beautiful ___! Where did you get it from?
  a sofa   c jewellery
  b furniture   d jeans

12 I know! I ___ up Uncle Francis in Salzburg.
  a will call   c will have called
  b am going to call   d will have been calling

13 ___ celebrities will stop at nothing to be in the limelight.
  a Any   c Some
  b No   d Much

14 ___ staying in Athens for long when the earthquake happened?
  a Had you   c You had been
  b Did you   d Had you been

15 They ___ their tour of Queensland by Sunday.
  a are finishing   c will be finishing
  b will have finished   d had been finishing

16 When ___ to build the roof garden?
  a are they going   c will they have been
  b they will   d they are going

17 Wow! There's so much ___ in this limousine!
  a spaces   c area
  b room   d rooms

18 Can you pick up a ___ of milk from the supermarket?
  a carton   c packet
  b bowl   d jar

19 Why are you carrying so ___ luggage?
  a many   c a lot of
  b lots of   d much

20 I ___ Constantinople until last year.
  a hadn't visited   c hadn't been visiting
  b wasn't visiting   d hadn't been visited

21 'Did you enjoy the concert?' 'By the time we arrived, the band ___ home.'
  a had went   c had gone
  b have went   d have gone

22 They had been waiting ___ five hours.
  a since   c yet
  b until   d for

23 She ___ my letter by now.
  a receives   c will be receiving
  b will have received   d will receive

24 I'd like ___ cheese and biscuits, please.
  a any   c some
  b few   d much

25 What are you ___ to study at university?
  a want   c having
  b will   d going

26 I was late because someone had ___ my car keys.
  a hided   c hiding
  b hidden   d hide

27 Not too ___ chocolate cake, please.
  a many   c much
  b lots   d few

28 Sorry, but I haven't got ___ cash.
  a no   c some
  b none   d any

Reading

A Read the *Exam Reminder*. What should you be cautious about?

_____

B Now complete the *Exam Task*.

MAYAN TECHNOLOGY

The ancient Maya, who lived in parts of present-day Central America, had a very sophisticated, complex civilisation and achieved remarkable things. By observing the skies they created a highly accurate calendar; they introduced new farming methods; and they managed to build spectacular temples and great cities without the use of metal or the wheel.

One of their greatest accomplishments was vulcanisation, which is the process of combining rubber with other materials to make it stronger and longer-lasting. Until recently, the discovery was credited to Charles Goodyear of the United States, who patented the technology in 1843. However, scientists and historians now believe that the Maya were producing rubber products from around 1600 BC – about 3,400 years before Goodyear. In fact, in the 16th century when Spanish explorers arrived in the area, they were astonished to see rubber balls, which were objects they had never encountered before. Even describing the stretchy, bouncy material proved difficult as it did not exist in Europe and was therefore beyond their experience.

It is believed that the Maya discovered this process by accident when they cooked latex from rubber trees with juice from a plant called morning glory. They quickly realised how strong the new material was and the wealth of things it could be used for: to line the soles of their sandals thus making them water resistant, as glue, and for the large rubber balls they used in the game known as pokatok played on stone-walled ball courts as part of a religious ceremony.

For questions **1 – 5** choose the answer (**a**, **b**, **c** or **d**) which fits best according to the text.

1 Which statement about the Maya is true?
  a They discovered Central America.
  b They did not know how to use the land.
  c Their temples were very complex.
  d They were good astronomers.

2 What do we learn about the Spanish?
  a They were at a loss for words.
  b They were inexperienced at ball games.
  c They went there looking for rubber.
  d They couldn't prove they'd seen rubber.

3 When is it believed rubber was initially used?
  a in 1843   **b** in 1600 BC
  c in 3400 BC   **d** in the 1500s

4 What did the Maya need for vulcanisation?
  a an accident with rubber
  b strong materials
  c two different materials and heat
  d high temperatures and glue

5 What did the Maya notice about rubber?
  a It was needed for religious ceremonies.
  b It made them wealthy.
  c It was good to build courts with.
  d It was tough and versatile.

Vocabulary

A Circle the odd one out.

1 lesson   lecture   excursion
2 evidence   proof   researcher
3 intelligent   harmful   addictive
4 permanent   limited   temporary
5 natural   lifelike   precise
6 fact   cost   price

B Complete the sentences with the correct form of the words.

1 There are many _____ exhibits on display in the museum.   **INTERACT**
2 Where do these stones _____ from?   **ORIGIN**
3 Fridges and cookers are common household _____.   **APPLY**
4 What time does the rocket _____ open at?   **EXHIBIT**
5 The flight _____ was an amazing experience.   **SIMULATE**
6 There have been many _____ advances over the past century.   **TECHNOLOGY**
7 _____ to radiation is extremely dangerous.   **EXPOSE**
8 Too much visual _____ isn't good for our brains.   **STIMULATE**

C Complete the text with these words.

ability   generate   lose   measure   miss   time machine

Travelling through time

Is it possible to travel to other eras either in the past or the future? If scientists have found an answer to this question, they're keeping quiet about it. However, the concept of a(n) (**1**) _____ is not a new one. In fact, it was as far back as 1895 that writer H G Wells published a short novel exploring this idea. In the novel, the main character is an inventor who has created a machine which has the (**2**) _____ to allow people to travel through time. During a dinner party, the inventor doesn't (**3**) _____ the opportunity to demonstrate his machine to his guests.

During the course of the experiment, the inventor travelled to far flung places and different eras. But how could he (**4**) _____ the success of the experiment? By looking at the clock, of course. He arrived back home three hours later. His guests were amazed by his stories, and so that they would not (**5**) _____ credibility, he even produced an unusual flower given to him by a creature he had met during his travels! The machine was sure to (**6**) _____ a lot of interest.

Grammar

Modals & Semi-modals

A Circle the correct words.

1 Could / May you take a look at my printer? It's broken.

2 She needn't / can't buy a DVD player because she doesn't have enough money.

3 You don't have to / shouldn't purchase electronic equipment that doesn't have a guarantee.

4 Will the technician can / be able to come tomorrow?

5 This must / can't be the website we were on earlier – it's completely different.

6 I oughtn't to / couldn't use a computer when I was fifteen.

7 You needn't / have to buy a new cable because we've got a spare one.

8 We should / ought to install photovoltaic panels.

B Complete the sentences by writing one word in each gap.

1 Wills _____ to wear his lab coat in the laboratory.

2 Will we be _____ to speak to the professor in person after the talk?

3 That girl _____ be Caroline's sister because she doesn't have one.

4 _____ I watch you doing the experiment?

5 They don't _____ to clean up after themselves; the cleaner does it.

6 You _____ buy that book because it's not for sale.

7 _____ Louise play video games when she was five?

8 You _____ not go near the reactor without protective clothing.

Listening

A Read the *Exam Reminder*. What is a helpful thing to do?

_____

B 5.1 ▶️ Listen and complete the *Exam Task*.

Exam Reminder

Choosing from pictures

- Always remember to look carefully at the pictures before listening, and think of words and expressions connected to each set.

- It's helpful to find a connection between the pictures and to think about a possible conversation.

- Try to also predict a possible question related to each set of pictures.

Exam Task

You will hear ten short conversations. After each conversation, you will be asked a question about what you heard. The answer choices are shown as pictures (**a**, **b** and **c**). Circle the letter of the correct answer. You hear each conversation only once.

C 5.1 ▶️ Listen again and check your answers.

Grammar

Perfect Modals

A Choose the correct answers.

1 Harry ought to have ___ for that IT job.
   a applied   b apply   c applying

2 ___ Gary have helped if we had asked him?
   a Should   b May   c Would

3 They ___ have tested the engine before putting it on the market.
   a ought   b must   c can

4 It ___ a doctor you spoke to earlier because there are no doctors here this week.
   a can't have been   b can't be   c couldn't be

5 You ___ warned us an electric storm was coming!
   a could have   b would have   c can

6 It was wrong to have launched the rocket yesterday – we ___ till tomorrow.
   a could wait   b must have waited   c should have waited

B Find and correct the mistakes in the sentences.

1 You mustn't have got me tickets to the planetarium; I've already got some. _____

2 They ought have told us the washing machine needed fixing. _____

3 Jan may have caused the fire because she wasn't here at the time. _____

4 Might I have asked permission before entering the laboratory? _____

5 The customers can have been impressed with the iPod because they have sold out! _____

6 Mark should have repaired the TV if you had asked him. _____

Use your English
Exam Task

For questions **1 – 10**, read the text below and think of a word which best fits each gap. Use only **one** word in each gap.

Some spare time activities

Spare time activities basically fall into two categories: traditional and modern. Traditional activities include pastimes such
(1) _____ collecting and reading while modern activities involve computer games, the Internet and television. Children often become interested **(2)** _____ collecting when they come **(3)** _____ something their parents or grandparents have collected. Although they are keen **(4)** _____ collecting when they first start, they very often become fed up with it as **(5)** _____ as they reach their late teens. Reading is a leisure activity that develops with parental encouragement. Unlike collecting, reading is a pastime that people hardly
(6) _____ abandon.

Nowadays **(7)** _____ are many modern activities which are based on modern technology, and it is not unusual to find a teenager's bedroom full **(8)** _____ computer games. While computer games
(9) _____ considered to be mainly a teenage pastime, surfing the Internet is popular with both teenagers and adults. Another pastime which teenagers have **(10)** _____ common with adults is watching television. It is interesting to note that none of these activities involve having a discussion about important issues – something which was popular in the past.

Exam Reminder

Filling the gaps
- Remember to read the whole text first to get a general understanding of it.
- Try to identify which part of speech is missing for each gap.
- Never leave any gaps unanswered.
- Don't forget to read the whole text again, checking the words you have written work well.

B For questions 1 – 10, read the text below and decide which answer (a, b, c or d) best fits each gap.

Recycling in the office

One of the most exciting new inventions in the field of recycling is a machine that can clean used photocopier paper. The device, (1) ___ a decopier, uses a mixture of chemicals to loosen the ink from the paper. A brush then (2) ___ the ink, leaving the paper completely clean. (3) ___ to the manufacturers, nothing like this has appeared on the (4) ___ before. They claim that the machine is (5) ___ of cleaning one sheet of paper at least five times. This is because the damage (6) ___ to the paper by the cleaning chemicals is compensated for by a special chemical which increases its (7) ___.

It is predicted that the machine will (8) ___ on despite the high cost. The initial price of £30,000 will be too high for small companies, but they will be able to (9) ___ one for a reasonable monthly sum, or wait for a cheaper version to (10) ___ out. Multinational companies will have a golden opportunity to help the environment and will save £30,000 within 18 months. What is more, the machine will, to a great extent, provide a way to improve security, as it offers an alternative to shredding confidential documents.

	a		b		c		d
1	called		named		known		described
2	rejects		resists		removes		refrains
3	Listening		Speaking		Accounting		According
4	shops		store		business		market
5	capable		able		possible		potential
6	made		exposed		inflicted		done
7	power		strength		health		fitness
8	catch		get		carry		bring
9	take		lend		borrow		rent
10	come		bring		go		get

C For questions 1 – 8, complete the second sentence so that it has a similar meaning to the first sentence, using the word given. Do not change the word given. You must use between two and five words, including the word given.

1 The telescope must be assembled before it gets dark.

better

They _____ the telescope before it gets dark.

2 I'm sure your holiday to New York was great.

been

Your holiday to New York _____ great.

3 She didn't switch off the computer because she forgot.

remember

She _____ off the computer.

4 It was wrong of you to leave the lecture before it ended.

ought

You _____ to the end of the lecture.

5 Don't set off without eating something first.

bite

You must _____ before you set off.

6 I don't think it was easy for him to leave his job.

can't

It _____ easy for him to leave his job.

7 Over 10,000 people are able to fit into this stadium.

seat

This stadium _____ over 10,000 people.

8 It's impossible for you to have seen Matt's brother because he doesn't have one.

have

It _____ Matt's brother you saw, because he doesn't have one.

Writing: an essay (1)

A Read the writing task below and answer the questions.

MODERN TALKING

In today's world, people communicate in all sorts of ways, however, personal contact seems to be taking more and more of a back seat. Without a doubt, modern technology has certainly had a huge influence on how people communicate. Be it text message, email or posts on social networking sites, the written word is often people's preferred means of communication these days. The editor of the City Times wants to know how people feel about this issue.

Essay

What do you think about the ways people communicate today? How have they affected our relationships? Have they had any negative effects?

1 What is the main topic of the essay?

2 How many things will you focus on in your essay?

3 What are they?

4 Should you express your own opinion? Why? / Why not?

Learning Reminder

Deciding what language to use in an essay

- When writing an essay, remember to read the task carefully and the essay topic to plan your writing. It's helpful to note down any topic-related vocabulary you might need.

- Organise your ideas into well-developed paragraphs and provide reasons and examples for your opinions. Also, use appropriate linking words and avoid extremely long sentences to make your writing flow well and easy to read.

- Don't forget to use formal language and avoid contractions and expressions which are more appropriate for spoken English.

B Read the example essay and cross out the linking word or phrase that cannot complete each item.

(1) According to / It is said / People often say that the way we communicate nowadays is much different to in the past. The question is, though, is this a change for the better?

These days, most people prefer to 'chat' on the Internet rather than meet in person. **(2)** For this reason / For example / Because of this, they have less real contact with others. **(3)** Although / In addition / Furthermore, there can be misunderstandings because a person's tone of voice cannot be expressed in writing and sometimes arguments result. **(4)** Thus / In spite of / Consequently, some people fear that personal relationships are suffering.

(5) On the other hand / Even though / However, others say modern means of communication **(6)** like / such / such as email and social networking sites have made communication simpler. They allow us to keep in touch with others at the touch of a button. **(7)** Even so / As a result / Therefore, it is much easier to keep relationships alive.

In my opinion, there are dangers of using modern technology to communicate. **(8)** Despite / In spite of / Though these dangers, I believe that if we use modern technology properly, it can help us build stronger relationships with those we care about.

C Read and complete the *Exam Task* below. Don't forget to use the *Useful Expressions* on page 67 of your Student's Book.

Exam Task

COMPUTER GAMES: ENTERTAINMENT OR A DANGER?

More and more people are becoming addicted to computer games. Researchers are worried about the effect this is having on their health as their eyesight may become poorer, they don't get enough physical exercise and they are more likely to suffer from depression than those who don't play these games. Also, personal relationships may be suffering. The editor of the City Times wants to know how people feel about this issue.

What do you think about computer games? Can they have any positive effects? How can we help those who have become addicted?

Write your **essay** in 140–190 words.

▶ Writing Reference p. 185 in Student's Book

6 Fun, Fun, Fun!

Reading

A Read the *Exam Reminder*. What should you do first?

_____

B Now complete the *Exam Task*.

Exam Reminder

Identifying the purpose of a text
- Firstly, identify the type of text you are reading. This will give you some idea of its purpose.
- When reading the text, decide who wrote it and who it's aimed at. This will give you more information about the text's purpose.
- Finally, read the text again carefully to decide what exactly the reason for writing it was.

A

> ◄ ► email
>
> **To:** All teachers
> **From:** sjmartin@school.com
> **Subject:** New ideas for summer programmes
>
> Dear Teachers,
>
> In response to the principal's request for suggestions regarding summer programmes, I would like to bring to your attention the International Youth Summer Games. They are the perfect opportunity for our students to meet teenagers from around the world. Here are some of the reasons why our students should take part in the games:
>
> - promote peace, friendship and understanding
> - all competitors receive medals
> - games will be held in our country this year
>
> I believe this is a worthwhile programme that our students will enjoy and learn from.
>
> Sincerely,
> Sarah J. Martin
> **Senior Teacher, Ferntree High School**

B

International Youth Summer Games

June 8th – June 15th

One of the world's premier youth sporting events is back! Teenagers from around the world will come together in the spirit of friendly competition. Day trips and activities such as cook-outs will give participants the chance to socialise and have fun.

How about this for fun?

- Novelty events like the tug of war, too!
- Opening ceremony; 'The Pins' sing their greatest hits!
- Over 2,000 athletes from 35 countries!

Participation is free for competitors
Visitors: $8 a day; under 18s $3

C

Can Sport Promote Peace?

Can sport make the world a more peaceful place? Yes, it can!

International events like the Olympics and the football World Cup bring people together in an atmosphere of peace. In fact, at the time of the ancient Olympics, hostilities ceased for the duration of the games, and the stated aim of the modern Olympics is to build a peaceful and better world.

So let's show our support for the young athletes of the International Youth Summer Games, currently being held in our city. Make it a fun day out for all the family.

Silverside Stadium, 10a.m. – 4 p.m. every day this week. Be there!

D

Profile: **Brian Thomas, athlete**

Brian Thomas is one of more than 2,000 young people who have come to Silverside to compete in the International Youth Summer Games. An annual event, the Games are held on a different continent each year.

Brian is really looking forward to the opening ceremony, which will take place in a few days. He says the ceremony is a huge party and a great way for the athletes to get to know each other. As this will be Brian's second games, he's very excited about catching up with teens he met last year in Sweden.

Although it is an international competition, athletes don't compete as national teams. Rather, each school that takes part forms its own team. For Brian, this means he's representing his school as a member of the boys' volleyball team. He has high hopes that his team will do well, but winning isn't everything. "We just love playing as a team. And you don't even have to be on a 'proper' team. You can just compete in the tug of war and have a blast!"

As a means of promoting world peace, it's very successful. "It's all about meeting people from around the world and seeing that there are more things that connect us than there are that divide us," said Brian.

Read the texts again. For questions **1 – 10**, choose the best answer (**a**, **b**, **c** or **d**).

1 What is the main purpose of text A?
  a to make a request
  b to suggest something
  c to promote an event
  d to explain something

2 What will happen on the first day of the event in text B?
  a There will be a cook-out.
  b About 2,000 people will be there.
  c There will be an excursion.
  d There will be a concert.

3 In text, B how much will athletes pay to take part?
  a $ 3   **b** $ 8
  c nothing   **d** $ 18

4 What does text C say happened during the ancient Olympics?
  a wars stopped
  b structures were built
  c lasting peace was restored
  d football was popular

5 Where would you most likely read text C?
  a in an email   **b** in a report
  c in a letter   **d** in a magazine

6 Which of the following is used as an example of a 'proper' team sport in text D?
  a tug of war   **b** water polo
  c hide and seek   **d** online gaming

7 Which country does text D say would not be able to host the Youth Games this year?
  a Peru   **b** Australia
  c Italy   **d** South Africa

8 In the last sentence of paragraph 3 in text D, what does have a blast mean?
  a enjoy yourself very much
  b pretend to fight
  c become very angry
  d launch a rocket

9 Which texts include information about team sports?
  a A, B and C   **b** A, B and D
  c A, C and D   **d** B, C and D

10 Which of the statements is true?
  a Brian is not from Silverside.
  b The events have not started yet.
  c There are no ticket discounts.
  d Everyone competes in the tug of war.

Vocabulary

A Complete the words in the sentences.

1 Ricky goes j _ _ _ _ _ _ along the seafront every morning.
2 Uma plays b _ _ _ _ _ _ _ _ _ in her spare time.
3 Unfortunately, they don't do a _ _ _ _ _ _ _ at the gym anymore.
4 We went w _ _ _ _ _ _ _ _ _ _ and kept falling into the water!
5 Let's play c _ _ _ _; I'll deal.
6 Cara is very fit because she does a _ _ _ _ _ _ _ _ every evening.
7 Doing g _ _ _ _ _ _ _ _ _ is a fun way to stay in shape.
8 You must wear a life-jacket to go s _ _ _ _ _ _ on the river.

C Choose the correct answers.

1 Is there an ice hockey __ near here?
  a ring   **b** pitch   **c** rink

2 I'll __ and deal the cards.
  a grab   **b** throw   **c** shuffle

3 Rio de Janeiro will __ the 2016 Olympic Games.
  a host   **b** beat   **c** award

4 Oh no! We forgot to bring the __ board!
  a cricket   **b** volleyball   **c** chess

B Complete the sentences with one word.

1 Let's go to the bowling _____ this evening.
2 Dad always heads for the golf _____ on Saturday mornings.
3 Who holds the world _____ for the high jump?
4 I play tennis from _____ to time.
5 There's a hotel in the middle of a motor racing _____ in Germany.
6 I'll surf the _____ to see if there are any good sports centres nearby.
7 Mary sprained her ankle on the squash _____.
8 I'm starving! Let's grab a _____ to eat.

5 And Murray is the first to __ the finishing line!
  a cross   **b** break   **c** browse

6 Why did Jones not __ up at the track?
  a run   **b** show   **c** feel

7 Sit __ and enjoy the show.
  a around   **b** together   **c** back

8 We're __ a party at the weekend.
  a turning   **b** throwing   **c** seating

Grammar

Gerunds & Infinitives

A Find and correct the mistakes in the sentences.

1 I joined the gym to getting fit. _____
2 To jog is a good way to stay in shape. _____
3 Do you enjoy to play basketball? _____
4 We had better buying the tickets in advance. _____
5 I'd rather going to the hockey match than the cinema. _____
6 During our walk, we stopped having a picnic at a lovely park. _____
7 Remember washing your kit before the next match! _____
8 The players were too tired give their best. _____

B Circle the correct words.

1 It's no use talking / to talk to Mary; she won't listen to you.
2 You were so lucky escape / to have escaped from the building during the earthquake.
3 It was so kind of you to take / taking me to hospital.
4 Could you get / to get tickets for the science fair?
5 The suspect denied knowing / to know anything about it.
6 Samantha couldn't afford going / to go on holiday this year.
7 You had better to hurry / hurry, or else you will miss the train.
8 Carol avoided driving / to drive in the rush hour when she lived in Paris.

Listening

A Read the *Exam Reminder*. What should you do once your answers are in place?

_____

B 6.1 ▶ Listen and complete the *Exam Task*.

Exam Reminder

Predicting the answer
- To predict answers, remember to look at the words before and after the gaps.
- Remember that you can use digits instead of writing numbers in their full form.
- Make sure you listen carefully to distinguish between teens and tens, e.g. 15 and 50.
- Make sure you also know the ordinal numbers.

Exam Task

You will hear a broadcast about the Edinburgh festival. For **1 – 10**, complete the sentences with a word or short phrase.

The Edinburgh Festival

The programme comes from one of Britain's (**1**) _____ enchanting cities. The presenter says there will be live reports once a week for a three-week period. The festival now (**2**) _____ contemporary dance performances taking centre stage, rather (**3**) _____ the usual Shakespeare plays, musicals and operas.

The box office is worth a visit. It is a beautiful spire and decorated inside (**4**) _____ contemporary art. People don't just go there to buy tickets, but also to hang (**5**) _____ with friends in the café.

The first festival was held in 1947, two years (**6**) _____ the end of World War II. It was decided that the arts was a good way for the city to get back on (**7**) _____ feet after the (**8**) _____.

Most venues are (**9**) _____ walking distance, so you don't have to get one the expensive taxis. For (**10**) _____, there are plenty of hotels, halls of residence, bed and breakfast and youth hostels. There's something for everyone at the festival.

C 6.1 ▶ Listen again and check your answers.

Grammar

Indirect Questions

A Complete the second sentences so that they have a similar meaning to the first sentences using the words in bold. Use between two and five words.

1 When does the boxing match end?

would

I _____ when the boxing match ends.

2 I wonder if you could take me to the concert tomorrow.

mind

Would _____ to the concert tomorrow?

3 I'd like to know how much the membership fee is.

suppose

I _____ how much the membership fee is.

4 Could I borrow your tennis racket?

lend

I wonder _____ your tennis racket.

5 Will you come to the dance with me?

ask

I'd _____ to come to the dance with me.

6 Could you help me carry this equipment?

wonder

I _____ me carry this equipment.

Question Tags

B Match the first half of the sentences 1 – 8 to the second half a – h.

1 That's Marty's hockey stick, ☐		a am I?
2 I'm going to win, ☐		b won't they?
3 They aren't on form today, ☐		c aren't they?
4 The coach was in a bad mood yesterday, ☐		d isn't it?
5 These are Todd's trainers, ☐		e aren't I?
6 I'm not in the team this year, ☐		f is she?
7 Chelsea will win the cup this year, ☐		g are they?
8 Martha isn't a full member, ☐		h wasn't she?

Use your English

A For questions 1 – 10, read the text below and think of the word which best fits each gap. Use only one word in each gap.

The history of vending machines

At some point in your life, you must (1) _____ used a vending machine. There can't (2) _____ a bus station, college campus or sports centre in the western world that doesn't have at least one machine. When you're on the move and don't have (3) _____ time to eat a meal, a snack from a vending machine can be just what you need. The first modern vending machine, (4) _____ was installed in London in the 1880s, didn't sell snacks though. Instead customers used the machine in (5) _____ to purchase postcards. Today's customers are (6) _____ to buy anything from packets of crisps to disposable toothbrushes from these handy machines. Most modern machines are electronic and must be plugged (7) _____, as a result they (8) _____ to have a power supply nearby. The very first vending machine, however, was not so hi-tech. It dates back to (9) _____ first century when engineer and mathematician Hero of Alexandria invented a coin-operated machine which (10) _____ pour water when a coin was placed on a lever. Even today it's the less complicated machines that are more profitable.

B For questions 1 – 10, read the text below and decide which answer (a, b, c or d) best fits each gap.

Student life

Congratulations! You've just been offered a place by the university of your choice. You've worked hard over the past few years and you deserve your success, but there are many more years of even harder work ahead. So how can you live up to your full (1) ___ and lead a balanced life during your student years? If you want to be (2) ___ your degree at the end of your course, you're obviously going to have to be disciplined enough to study (3) ___ time to time! You'll also have to attend and pay attention in (4) ___. However, it doesn't need to be all boring academics! There's nothing better for students than becoming (5) ___ at the uni gym. Not only will (6) ___ jogging round the athletics (7) ___ keep you fit, but it will also help you to concentrate on your studies and make you more disciplined. The same goes for team sports and other forms of physical exercise like doing (8) ___. Whenever you don't feel (9) ___ to studying, head for the gym and you'll find after a good workout that you're in a better frame of mind to write that assignment that must be handed in at the end of the week. Try to get into a fitness routine rather than just working out when you're at a (10) ___ end. Even during the holidays when it's tempting to sit around all day doing nothing, stick to your fitness routine. If the gym is closed, go for a brisk walk in your neighbourhood. Remember *A healthy mind in a healthy body* means that staying fit will help you achieve academic success.

1	a	ability	b	potential	c	lesson	d	tension	6	a	going	b	playing	c	doing	d	running
2	a	awarded	b	presented	c	rewarded	d	held	7	a	course	b	track	c	ring	d	field
3	a	in	b	on	c	with	d	from	8	a	basketball	b	golf	c	aerobics	d	volleyball
4	a	sessions	b	excursions	c	lectures	d	exhibitions	9	a	up	b	down	c	into	d	for
5	a	interactive	b	lifelike	c	intelligent	d	active	10	a	limited	b	harmful	c	loose	d	blue

C Complete the *Exam Task*.

Exam Task

For questions 1 – 10, read the text below. Use the word given in capitals at the end of some of the lines to form a word that fits in the gap in the same line.

Welcome to Buddingartists.com, an (1) _____ web page designed to provide   INTERACT
tutorials for artists from absolute (2) _____ to advanced students. Read the   BEGIN
reviews previous (3) _____ have written about our courses – you'll see that the   PARTICIPATE
tutorials became an (4) _____ for most of them. Follow the link for the Students'   ADDICT
Gallery to browse our students' (5) _____. You'll be impressed at the quality of all   COLLECT
works.

Many of our former students have even gone on to become established artists participating in group
and solo (6) _____ at some of the most prestigious galleries in the world.   EXHIBIT

So why join Buddingartists.com? Creating works of art is a hobby which you can enjoy anywhere and
it doesn't require expensive (7) _____. Our tutorials teach you how to study your   EQUIP
subject – a much needed skill in today's world where constant (8) _____   EXPOSE
to images often leads to our visual awareness being overloaded as we receive too much
(9) _____ from TV, adverts, etc. So what are you waiting for? Nurture your artistic   STIMULATE
(10) _____ and sign up for a course that suits you. Free 15-day trial for all new users.   ABLE

Writing: a report

A Read the writing task below and write T (true) or F (false).

> You work at a sports centre. Your manager wants to attract more members to the sports centre and has asked you to write a report. Your report should cover the sports on offer, the membership fee and the facilities, and anything else you consider relevant.

Organising paragraphs
- Remember to organise your report clearly and include introductory information about the subject, the identity of the writer and the recipient.
- Then follow on with an introduction, a main body and a conclusion.
- Each paragraph in the main body should have a heading and you should state your recommendations in the conclusion.

Write your **report** in 140–190 words in an appropriate style.

1 You are the manager of a sports centre. ☐
2 Your report should heavily criticise the sports centre. ☐
3 The purpose of the report is to inform the manager about what people think about the sports centre. ☐
4 Your report will discuss three main points. ☐
5 Recommendations will be included in the conclusion. ☐

B Read the example report and write the headings below in the appropriate places and circle the correct phrases and sentences.

Facilities   Conclusion   Sports offered   Introduction   Cost of Membership

To: Kay Green, Manager
From: Duncan Sheldon
Subject: Report on Grand Slam Sports Centre

(a) _____
This report is intended to suggest ways in which the sports centre can attract more members. I spoke with a number of members and (**1**) this is what they had to say / my findings are presented below.

(b) _____
Almost everyone agreed that the sports centre should offer non-competitive sports as well as sports like football, basketball and volleyball. (**2**) How about starting up tai chi and yoga? /
In particular, members are keen to have classes in tai chi and yoga.

(c) _____
The majority of people thought that the membership fee is too high, and that some people cannot join the sports centre as a result. (**3**) You've got to / The most popular suggestion was to reduce the membership fee and offer a family discount.

(d) _____
(**4**) Regarding / Now, about general facilities, most people would like there to be more changing rooms as
(**5**) it's shocking how few there are / there are not enough at the moment. One idea would be to make the cafeteria smaller in order to extend the current changing rooms.

(e) _____
(**6**) So, make membership fees cheaper / I would therefore suggest that membership fees be more affordable especially for families. Also, it would be a good idea to introduce non-competitive sports and create more changing facilities.

C Read and complete the *Exam Task* below. Don't forget to use the *Useful Expressions* on page 79 of your Student's Book.

Exam Task

> You work part-time at a skating rink. Your supervisor has asked you to write a report following recent complaints. Your report should cover health and safety, opening hours and special offers, and anything else you consider relevant.

Write your **report** in 140–190 words in an appropriate style.

↻ Writing Reference p. 184 in Student's Book

Vocabulary

A Choose the correct answers.

1 A new recycling ___ is being built outside town.
a pack   c plant
b rink   d court

2 And Milan ___ Manchester United 3-0!
a win   c award
b beat   d reward

3 Those kids get too much ___ to TV.
a exposure   c information
b addiction   d simulation

4 Let's go to the bowling ___ after work.
a pitch   c machine
b session   d alley

5 You ___ the cards and I'll deal.
a share   c host
b shuffle   d measure

6 The judge put the ___ round the winner's neck.
a prize   c medal
b exhibit   d gear

7 I'm in two ___ about going to the science fair.
a moons   c paths
b thoughts   d minds

8 Brandon ___ the finishing line second.
a crossed   c steered
b broke   d pulled

9 Is it easy to ___ into a Facebook account?
a hook   c browse
b switch   d hack

10 These solar panels can ___ enough hot water for the whole family.
a sample   c generate
b navigate   d assemble

11 Why didn't you show ___ for the party?
a up to   c into
b in   d up

12 Mum ___ aerobics at the gym.
a plays   c does
b goes   d makes

13 Diana makes clothes on her ___ machine.
a sewing   c vending
b washing   d time

14 Hurry or we'll ___ the electronics lecture.
a lose   c press
b miss   d stroll

15 These model dinosaurs look so ___!
a lifelike   c connected
b enjoyable   d improved

16 Read the instruction ___ to connect the printer.
a bolt   c manual
b venue   d collection

17 Shall we ___ a bite to eat?
a grab   c treat
b sip   d fancy

18 The Internet is an amazing ___ advance.
a natural   c unappealing
b technological   d portable

19 They plan to ___ the rocket next month.
a set off   c launch
b input   d lounge

20 ___ back and enjoy the show.
a Seat   c Feel
b Sit   d Get

21 Joe doesn't ___ up to going back to school yet.
a feel   c look
b make   d live

22 Do you remember how to ___ in to your IT account?
a log   c key
b go   d turn

23 I left a message on your answering ___ last night.
a box   c machine
b phone   d engine

24 Why did he turn ___ the job?
a up   c down
b off   d around

25 We missed the flight because we slept ___.
a in   c under
b on   d over

26 Let's all get ___ for a coffee and a chat sometime this week.
a in   c about
b around   d together

27 somebody has hacked ___ my computer and stolen my passwords
a over   c into
b on   d off

28 Turn ___ the music. I can't hear it!
a down   c out
b off   d up

Grammar

B **Choose the correct answers.**

1 You ___ take up a new hobby if you're bored.
   a ought   **c** should
   b might   **d** are able to

2 This is Jay's iPhone, ___?
   a is it   **c** isn't this
   b isn't she   **d** isn't it

3 Why ___ turn up for practice? We missed you.
   a you didn't   **c** did you
   b didn't you   **d** weren't you

4 It's not worth ___ all your money on a car.
   a spending   **c** to spend
   b spend   **d** for spending

5 He might ___ us he wasn't coming to the game.
   a tell   **c** be telling
   b have told   **d** tells

6 ___ can harm the joints.
   a To jog   **c** Jogging
   b Jog   **d** Jogged

7 We ___ to be at the stadium before 6 pm.
   a have   **c** should
   b must   **d** may

8 It ___ have been Jo you saw in town; he's in Rio.
   a must   **c** can
   b mustn't   **d** can't

9 It wasn't your bag that got stolen, ___ it?
   a was   **c** were
   b is   **d** wasn't

10 I don't ___ you could tell me where the bank is.
   a wonder   **c** like to know
   b suppose   **d** mind

11 The marathon should ___ hours ago.
   a finish   **c** have finished
   b finished   **d** finishing

12 They weren't pleased ___ their team lost.
   a hearing   **c** to hear
   b hear   **d** with hearing

13 ___ you help me pick out a new cricket bat?
   a Could   **c** Would you mind
   b I don't suppose   **d** I wonder

14 We won't know the winner till later, ___ we?
   a do   **c** will
   b shall   **d** have

15 The technician ___ fix the problem yesterday.
   a can   **c** have
   b was able to   **d** could

16 Would Bertie rather ___ football or play football?
   a watching   **c** he watches
   b to watch   **d** watch

17 You ___ have got me a ticket as I already have one.
   a needn't   **c** should
   b mustn't   **d** couldn't

18 They ___ to have put a fence round the pool.
   a ought   **c** might
   b have   **d** should

19 I'm next, ___ I?
   a am not   **c** are
   b aren't   **d** isn't

20 Do you ___ if I borrow your laptop?
   a wonder   **c** like
   b suppose   **d** mind

21 Samantha should never ___ married that man.
   a have   **c** been
   b had   **d** of

22 Those ships are all from the same country, ___?
   a aren't they   **c** they are
   b aren't those   **d** those aren't

23 Let's have a game of tennis, ___?
   a have we   **c** will we
   b let we   **d** shall we

24 When we were young, we ___ climb trees.
   a used   **c** may
   b would   **d** should

25 You ___ have bothered asking, he was always going to say 'no'.
   a couldn't   **c** needn't
   b should   **d** didn't

26 You really ___ to study a bit harder.
   a should   **c** must
   b ought   **d** could

27 Toby's a careless rider, ___?.
   a is he   **c** isn't he
   b does he   **d** hasn't he

28 I think she'd rather ___ out than stay home.
   a to go   **c** going
   b go   **d** went

Reading

A Read the *Exam Reminder*. What do common distractors use?

_____

B Now complete the *Exam Task*.

Restorative youth justice –

the way forward for youth offenders?

Preventing youth offenders from re-offending is one of the most difficult issues facing those involved in handing out punishments to 10-17 year olds. Prisons and rehabilitation centres have long been recognised as finishing schools for young inmates. Many youths enter these institutions as the perpetrators of petty crimes such as burglary, yet often they leave having acquired good fighting skills and knowledge of illegal activities such as drug dealing.

It is no great secret that for the majority of juvenile offenders, rehabilitation centres and youth prisons are ineffective and inadequate. Herding offenders together only gives them the chance to learn from each other. Those who have been put away for having committed minor offences are very often held in the same prisons as those who have committed serious offences such as murder and been found guilty by a jury. Given that the only other people their age that they can interact with are other offenders, inmates are obviously exposed to 'bad influences'. In this sense, these institutions are often a breeding ground for the ever-increasing adult population of criminals.

It's little wonder that many governments are seeking a more effective option to punishing and rehabilitating young offenders. In Northern Ireland, an organisation called the Youth Justice Agency was set up in 2003 with the aim of reducing the number of children in prisons. They introduced a method called *line 24* restorative youth justice in the belief that this could be the key to true rehabilitation.

At the very heart of restorative youth justice is a basic principle: offenders must make amends for their crimes and if possible, face their victims. This groundbreaking programme focuses not only on punishing the perpetrators of crime, but also on helping their victims. Each offender has to attend a structured youth conference along with family and community members, as well as a police officer. During this conference, the victim of the crime has the opportunity to tell the offender how he or she suffered due to the crime and how this has affected his or life. Although this takes tremendous courage on the victim's part, it usually has impressive results with the offender being more likely to show remorse and regret for his or her actions.

During the conference, an action plan is established for the offender. This usually involves several stages and various activities. For example, the offender is asked to apologise either in person or in writing to those directly affected by the crime. Also, they are asked to do something for the victim or for society in general to make up for the harm they have caused. This often entails payment of compensation. They are also put on an offender behaviour programme which means that they will be offered mentoring in order to prevent them from re-offending. Young offenders are also supervised by a social worker to help keep the rehabilitation process on track and, if there is a history of alcohol or drug addiction or mental health problems, they are given suitable treatment. In certain cases, offenders may also have to do unpaid work for up to 240 hours. Finally, restrictions may be placed on young offenders including where they are allowed to go, what they are allowed to do and whose company they are allowed to keep.

The Northern Ireland experiment gives hope for the future. In 2006, under 38% of young offenders who were dealt with through this system went on to offend once again. This is a vast improvement if we consider that in the same year over 52% of offenders who were simply given community service and over 70% of offenders who were given a prison sentence re-offended.

You are going to read an article about young offenders. For questions **1 – 6**, choose the answer (**a, b, c** or **d**) which you think fits best according to the text.

1 In prisons and rehabilitation centres, young offenders can
  a buy and sell drugs freely.
  b pick up bad habits.
  c finish their education.
  d learn invaluable skills.

2 The writer says that giving young offenders a prison sentence
  a helps to rehabilitate them.
  b should only happen for very serious crimes.
  c doesn't have the desired affect for most offenders.
  d results in all offenders turning to a life of crime when released.

3 What does 'They' in paragraph 3, line 24 refer to?
  a children in prisons
  b governments
  c young offenders
  d the Youth Justice Agency

4 The main aim of restorative youth justice is to
  a help offenders make up for their crimes.
  b severely punish young offenders.
  c help victims of youth crimes.
  d create a better relationship between victims and offenders.

5 Structured youth conferences
  a end with offenders receiving one specific punishment.
  b allow victims to help create an action plan for offenders.
  c require offenders to show a lot of courage.
  d result in a programme for dealing with the offender being drawn up.

6 The Northern Ireland example proves that
  a community service is totally ineffective in rehabilitating offenders.
  b restorative youth justice is an improvement over other ways of dealing with offenders.
  c prison sentences among youths are on the increase.
  d restorative youth justice is a complete success.

Vocabulary

A Match the first parts of the sentences 1 – 6 to the second parts a – f.

1 I advised my client to plead ☐   **a** a statement later today.
2 Clark always claimed that he had been falsely ☐   **b** held next month.
3 The hijacker's lawyer will make ☐   **c** a fine for polluting the river.
4 A hearing will be ☐   **d** guilty of assault.
5 The jury finally reached ☐   **e** accused of stealing.
6 The company has to pay ☐   **f** a verdict after 48 hours.

B The words in bold are in the wrong sentences. Write each word next to the correct sentence.

1 It was the first time the judge had tried such a difficult **court**. _____

2 Everyone knew they were hardened **clothes** and kept away from them. _____

3 He was arrested for handling stolen **criminals**. _____

4 The plain **case** police officer went undetected in the gang. _____

5 Sharon was taken to **goods** and tried for shoplifting. _____

6 Smoking in public places is a criminal **service** in many countries. _____

7 Tod was given 200 hours of community **duty** for arson. _____

8 I wish I hadn't been chosen to do jury **act**. _____

C Choose the correct answers.

1 Who is the main _____ for the crime?
  a suspect   **b** terrorist   **c** kidnapper

2 If you _____ yourself up, you'll receive a reduced sentence.
  a hold   **b** give   **c** get

3 After four years in prison, Gary is being _____ free next week.
  a let   **b** released   **c** set

4 She claimed that she acted in _____ when she shot the man.
  a self-defence   **b** prison   **c** sight

5 The burglar stayed hidden _____ sight until the family went out.
  a in   **b** of   **c** from

6 Most western countries there are a lot of policemen in _____ clothes.
  a uniform   **b** normal   **c** plain

Grammar

Passive Voice

A Complete the sentences with the correct passive form of these verbs.

| arrest | break into | call | knock down | print | release | sentence | start |

1 Grant _____ to five years in a high-security prison.
2 The fire _____ by arsonists.
3 An article on victims of violent crimes _____ in tomorrow's paper.
4 Our school _____ four times this term!
5 During court cases, witnesses _____ to give evidence.
6 Look! That actor _____ by a police officer!
7 The murderer mustn't _____ from prison!
8 The old lady _____ by a reckless driver at the weekend.

B Complete the text by writing one word in each gap.

Holly Police Station Log

24th December

At 11 pm an elderly gentleman wearing a Santa suit and a young lady wearing an elf's costume (1) _____ brought into the station by Officers Mistle and Toe. The man had (2) _____ caught trying to break into a residence on Laplan Road by climbing down the chimney. The large sack the man was carrying at the time was (3) _____ by the officers and it (4) _____ found to contain gifts which (5) _____ been wrapped in shiny paper. The gifts also had gift tags with the names of the occupants of the house written on them. The occupants, who had been asleep, were (6) _____ up by all the noise outside. They all denied having seen the gifts before. While the burglars were (7) _____ questioned at the station, they both seemed very nervous and kept talking about other 'deliveries'. The man claimed that he had been trying to leave presents for the family when he (8) _____ seen by the officers. A handwriting specialist has (9) _____ called in to analyse the writing on the cards and a handwriting sample which was given to the officers (10) _____ both suspects.

Listening

A Read the *Exam Reminder*. What is unlikely to happen?

_____

B 🔊 7.1 Listen and complete the *Exam Task*.

Exam Reminder

Expressing feelings through words
- Try to pay attention to how someone expresses themselves when the question asks about feelings.
- Remember the words a person uses to express his/her feelings are important.
- Don't forget that a person is unlikely to express themselves in the exact words used in the options.

Exam Task

You will hear people talking in seven situations. For questions 1 – 7, choose the best answer, (a, b or c).

1 You hear a woman talking. How does she feel about going back to university?
   a challenged
   b excited
   c nervous

2 You hear a teenager talking to a friend. Why is he talking to her?
   a to convince her to shoplift
   b to admit to having just stolen something
   c to complain about the prices in the shop

3 You hear a radio interview. Why did the man choose a life of crime?
   a He hated school.
   b He got pleasure from breaking the law.
   c He couldn't relate to his teachers.

4 You hear a man talking to his daughter. What is he worried about?
   a that his daughter hasn't made any friends yet
   b that his daughter has been breaking the law
   c that his daughter's friend may be a bad influence on her

5 You hear a man talking on the radio. What is he?
   a a judge   b a lawyer   c a member of the jury

6 You hear a prison warden talking. What does she imply about her job?
   a It's extremely dangerous.
   b It's very rewarding.
   c It's always difficult.

7 You hear a man talking. Why did he hit a teenager?
   a for stealing his car
   b in self-defence
   c because he didn't like his appearance

C 🔊 7.1 Listen again and check your answers.

Grammar

Causative

A Match the first half of the sentences 1 – 6 to the second half a – f.

1 You should have a burglar alarm ☐   **a** to approach the suspicious couple.
2 Karen had her windows ☐   **b** knocked out in a fight.
3 They got the police ☐   **c** smashed by some youths.
4 The lawyer is getting her assistant ☐   **d** thrown at her as she left court.
5 He had his front teeth ☐   **e** installed at the shop.
6 The judge had yoghurt ☐   **f** to research the case.

B Complete the sentences using the causative form of the verbs in brackets.

1 They _____ by this time next week. (the police station / decorate)
2 Gary always _____ the contracts. (his lawyer / check)
3 Why _____ she _____ in her living room last year? (hidden cameras / install)
4 The prisoner _____ by the guards at the moment. (his cell / search)
5 He _____ his gun. (the bank robber / put down)
6 We _____ three times already! (our garden table / steal)

Use your English

A For questions 1 – 8, read the text below and decide which answer (a, b, c or d) best fits each gap.

When people (1) _____ the law, they very rarely consider the consequences of their actions. Most criminals don't think about their victims and many believe they will never get caught and be (2) _____ away for their crimes. Even when they are placed (3) _____ arrest and accused (4) _____ committing a crime, some criminals still believe that they won't be found guilty. They live for the moment and enjoy the thrill of doing something that is against the law. They almost never stop to think what having a criminal (5) _____ might mean for their future. This attitude is partly the reason why some people choose to lead a life (6) _____ crime. Even when they are caught, few criminals confess to (7) _____ crimes. Some criminals are even convinced that because they have had a difficult life, they somehow deserve to make their living dishonestly. When (8) _____ a bank, for instance, a criminal may be totally convinced that all banks are corrupt and, therefore, might believe it's his or her duty to take the money. They give little or no thought to the people whose money it is that they are stealing.

1 a break	**b** believe	**c** think	**d** give	**5 a** file	**b** record	**c** accusation	**d** court
2 a closed	**b** put	**c** found	**d** brought	**6 a** to	**b** of	**c** with	**d** at
3 a in	**b** at	**c** of	**d** under	**7 a** their	**b** his	**c** our	**d** her
4 a for	**b** of	**c** on	**d** against	**8 a** rob	**b** steal	**c** robbing	**d** stealing

B Complete the text with the correct form of the words.

The toilet roll bandits

Two (1) _____ men were arrested in Rutherglen Main Street following an   **MASK**
(2) _____ robbery at a restaurant in the town. A witness to the crime made the   **ARM**
following (3) _____: 'I was coming out of the butcher's when I saw the   **STATE**
(4) _____ running out of the restaurant with their faces covered with toilet roll.   **ROB**
At first I thought it was a joke, but when I noticed they were carrying (5) _____   **DEAD**
weapons, it dawned on me it was no laughing matter!' The two men were taken to Rutherglen Police
Station where it was discovered they both had (6) _____ records. One of the   **CRIME**
men is a known (7) _____ in the Rutherglen area with five previous convictions and   **MUG**
is considered a (8) _____ criminal by locals. Their case is due to be   **HARD**
(9) _____ next week at the Magistrates' Court. A stunned employee said, 'I was   **TRY**
scared out of my wits. I hope they get a prison sentence this time. Punishments like community
(10) _____ are far too lenient for these kinds of criminals.'   **SERVE**

C **Now complete the *Exam Task*.**

For questions **1 – 8**, complete the second sentence so that it has a similar meaning to the first sentence, using the word given. **Do not change the word given.** You must use between **two** and **five** words, including the word given.

1 The emergency services evacuated all the residents after the hurricane.
by
After the hurricane, all the residents [writing line] the emergency services.

2 They are going to demolish the old shoe factory next month.
pulled
The old shoe factory is _____ next month.

3 The police officer questioned the burglar after robbery.
was
The burglar _____ the police officer after the robbery.

4 They are engraving numbers on the tortoise's shell.
is
The tortoise _____ on its shell.

5 The jury reached a verdict of not guilty for the accused.
found
The accused _____ the jury.

6 He is getting out of prison tomorrow.
from
They _____ prison tomorrow.

7 I didn't realise you were a bank robber!
of
I _____ the fact you were a bank robber!

8 Someone stole my car last night.
had
I _____ last night.

writing: a formal letter

A **Read the writing task below and answer the questions.**

Neighbourhood Watch

A group of residents in Blackton have decided enough is enough when it comes to crime. Given the recent increase in crimes such as vandalism, burglary and joyriding, these residents have formed a Neighbourhood Watch group. Members of this group take turns to patrol the streets and are always on the look-out for suspicious people in the area. The editor of the *Blackton Reformer* would like to know your views on this.

Letter

Should residents get involved in police work? Write a letter to the editor to explain your view. Give specific examples of why Neighbourhood Watch schemes are or aren't a good idea. Start your letter, 'Dear Editor'.

1 What have Blackton residents done?

2 Why did they think this was necessary?

3 Which question should your letter answer?

4 What should you include in your letter?

5 Do you think Neighbourhood Watch schemes are a good idea? Why/Why not?

B Read the example letter and write the topic sentences below in the correct paragraph. Then write how the writer's opinions are the same as or different to your own.

However, I disagree that ordinary citizens should get involved in police work.

I disagree with the view that if the police cannot reduce crime, the local people should help out.

I read your article about the Neighbourhood Watch scheme that has been set up by the residents of Blackton.

In short, I believe that creating groups like the one in Blackton is not the best way to tackle neighbourhood crime.

Dear Editor,

(1) _____

_____

I sympathise with these residents and fully understand how distressing it must be to live in an area with a high crime rate. It is very unfortunate that in our times, some people do not feel safe in their own homes.

(2) _____

_____

Reporting crimes to police that residents happen to witness is one thing, but patrolling the streets is quite another. These people are putting themselves at risk, for this reason I cannot support Neighbourhood Watch groups.

(3) _____

_____

To my mind, it would be better if these people protested to the local authorities about inadequate policing in their area. That way proper action could be taken by those responsible for crime prevention.

(4) _____

_____

Law and order is a matter for the authorities and it can be dangerous for ordinary citizens to get involved in police work.

---

a I agree that _____.

b I disagree that _____.

C Read and complete the *Exam Task* below. Don't forget to use the *Useful Expressions* on page 93 of your Student's Book.

Exam Task

Police officer sprays students with pepper spray

At a peaceful student protest, a police officer sprayed dangerous pepper spray directly into the faces of students who refused to move from the university campus. This action has angered many people as it was completely unprovoked. The editor of the *Carlton Times* would like to know your views on this.

Letter

Should the police be allowed to use weapons against demonstrators? Write a letter to the editor to explain your view. Give specific examples of what the consequences of using such weapons might be. Start your letter, 'Dear Editor'.

Write your **letter** in approximately 150 words.

Writing Reference p. 179 in Student's Book

Reading

A Read the *Exam Reminder*. What can linking words help you to do?

_____

B Now complete the *Exam Task*.

Exam Reminder

Identifying linking words in a text
- Remember that linking words can help to work out where to place missing sentences.
- Try to find the language in the missing sentences that refers back to the text.
- When you are looking for the linking words in the text, don't forget that they are often articles, pronouns or time clauses.

Help the environment get into shape with the
360° Energy Diet!

We are all too aware that our environment isn't in the best of health. We're constantly being asked to reduce our carbon footprint, though few of us understand what this means in practical terms. **1 [ ]**

Like all diets, the 360° Energy Diet is based on sacrifices - often very difficult sacrifices. However, the diet is structured in such a way that it's relatively easy to identify problem areas that your household needs to work on, and to keep a record of how well you are progressing. **2 [ ]** They are What you buy, Food, Transportation, At home, Water use, and finally, Waste disposal and reduction. Let's look at each of these categories in detail.

In Category 1, What you buy, dieters are encouraged to take a long hard look at utilities they pay for. Even small reductions in how much electricity, gas and water we use can make a huge difference to the environment as well as to our bank accounts. Dieters are also advised to look at their shopping baskets and, each week, to replace three items with organic equivalents and to eliminate three cleaning products with a high chemical content with three environmentally friendly ones. **3 [ ]** Imported produce comes under fire given the huge amounts of carbon dioxide that is produced flying and shipping goods from the other side of the world.

Food is category 2 in the diet, and for many, the most difficult category to stick to. **4 [ ]** Even more points are awarded if they can avoid all animal products and eat vegan or raw food only. If that seems like a tall order, just reducing your intake of beef can ensure that less tropical forest needs to be cut down to graze cattle.

Category 3 is Transportation. Without a doubt, we can all reduce the number of journeys we make using carbon dioxide-producing means such as private cars and opt for public transport, walking or cycling. For those journeys where cars are essential, dieters are encouraged to reduce the amount of petrol they consume by driving slowly and removing extra weight from the car such as heavy items on roof racks and in boots. Extra points can be gained if you can car pool or swap your high-consumption vehicle for a more energy-efficient model.

5 [ ] Make simple changes like lowering the thermostat on your heating system, changing your fridge settings and replacing ordinary light bulbs with LED bulbs in order to make huge energy savings. But probably the biggest difference can be made by not only switching off unused electrical appliances, but also by unplugging them from the mains.

Be aware of how much water is used by the household and strive to reduce this amount is what Category 5 demands of dieters. **6 [ ]** You should also reduce the time you spend in the shower and give up your power shower for a low-flow nozzle.

Last but not least is Category 6, Waste disposal and reduction. Here the advice is simple: reduce, reuse and recycle. Recycle glass, aluminium, plastic and paper, as well as electronic equipment in order to cut down on the amount of waste that ends up in landfills. When you go to the supermarket, don't forget to take reusable bags to avoid environmentally unfriendly plastic bags.

All these ideas may seem like common sense, but it's surprising how few of us put them into practice on a regular basis. If you feel the time has come for change in your house, then put everyone on the 360° Energy Diet. **7 [ ]**

Seven sentences have been removed from the text. Choose from the sentences **A – H** the ones which fits each gap (**1 – 7**). There is one extra sentence which you do not need to use.

A But energy efficiency should start in the home, and that's what the next category covers.

B This can be easily achieved by using filtered tap water instead of bottled.

C Buying locally will gain you more points on the 360° Energy Diet.

D Install solar or photovoltaic panels where possible.

E In the long run, we'll all reap the rewards.

F If the latter rings a bell, then the 360° Energy Diet might be exactly what you need.

G Dieters are encouraged to go vegetarian at least one day a week.

H The diet, which is based on a point system, is divided into six broad categories.

Vocabulary

A **Complete the sentences by writing one word in each gap.**

1 Young children should be discouraged _____ throwing rubbish in the street.

2 Can the rescue agency cope _____ all the victims?

3 If rock erodes, it _____ away.

4 I'm not keen _____ going on an eco-holiday.

5 The ecosystem of the Amazon has suffered badly due to _____.

6 It was a damp morning and the cars were covered in _____.

7 We can rely _____ Brian to help us clean up the beach.

8 Don't go out in that _____ rain.

B **Complete the text with these words.**

> climate change   conservation   ecosystems   endangered species   objected   resulted   victims   wiped

Is the panda worth saving?

Out of all (**1**) _____, the panda must be the most endearing. Native to China, these adorable black and white bears have long been (**2**) _____ of disease and (**3**) _____. They have also evolved from carnivores into herbivores, which has (**4**) _____ in a weakening of the species. Without attempts at the (**5**) _____ of this species, pandas would probably have been (**6**) _____ out long ago. However, some conservationists feel that maybe the time has come to say 'goodbye' to the panda. Some claim that for too long we have searched for funds to save just one species. Instead, we should be focusing on trying to save whole (**7**) _____ like the Amazon. While other conservationists agree that we need to look at the bigger picture, they have (**8**) _____ to completely abandoning the panda for this very reason. They claim that we should be focusing our efforts on saving the panda's natural habitat, which is also home to other rare species, such as the golden monkey and the red panda.

C **Circle the odd one out.**

1	rainfall	wind turbine	downpour
2	cycle	drought	global warming
3	delta	gust	river bank

4	flames	natural gas	crude oil
5	agriculture	fertilisers	current
6	sea level	fossil fuels	natural resources

D **Circle the correct words.**

1 There has been a rise / threat in temperatures in recent years.

2 I have great protection / respect for conservationists.

3 You ought to try to eat more biological / organic produce.

4 This car only runs on environmentally-friendly / unleaded petrol.

5 The local residents were exposed / aware to radiation after the explosion.

6 Are you pessimistic / satisfied about the future of the planet?

7 The perfume will evaporate / consume if you leave the bottle open.

8 Climate change is caused by natural habitats / forces and human activity.

Grammar

Conditionals: Zero, First, Second & Third

A Find and correct the mistakes in the sentences. Sometimes there is more than one answer.

1 If I were you, I will sign the petition. _____

2 If the sun sets, thousands of mosquitoes appeared. _____

3 If they hadn't gone on the demonstration, they wouldn't have being injured. _____

4 If the utilities company would pay me well, I'll sell them the electricity these panels generate.
_____

5 If they banned cars from the city centre, there will be less pollution. _____

6 If the temperature rises further, the ice-caps would have melted. _____

7 Would you study environmental issues if they had offered a course on it? _____

8 If we recycle paper, aluminium, glass and plastic, we would help the environment. _____

B Complete the text with the correct conditional form of these verbs.

> be   consume   notice   not know   prove   save   use   want

Power showers – money down the drain?

If you (1) _____ already _____, environmentalists usually promote showers over baths. They claim that much less water is consumed by showering than bathing. If you try to fill up your bath tub, you (2) _____ that it takes much longer to fill it up than it does to have a shower. Therefore, you (3) _____ more water if you leave the tap running to fill up the tub. In Britain, that nation of bath-lovers, it has been estimated that if every person took one less bath per week, the total savings (4) _____ equivalent to the water used per year in 15000 homes. In recent years, more and more people are opting for showers. However, it has recently been claimed that showering might not necessarily lead to lower water consumption. For instance, if you have a power shower in your bathroom and take showers lasting over five minutes, it (5) _____ up more water than a bath. If you (6) _____ to check this out for yourself, you can do a simple experiment. The next time you take a power shower, put in the bath plug to see how much water you actually use. You might be surprised to see that the bath will overflow. If your experiment (7) _____ this theory, you might consider swapping your power shower for a low-flow one. You can even take it one stage further for extra savings. If you reduce the time you spend showering by just one minute, you (8) _____ over 3000 litres of water a year.

Listening

A Read the Exam Reminder. Why is it important to concentrate on why someone is speaking?

_____

B 8.1 ▶️ Listen and complete the Exam Task.

Exam Task

You will hear five people speaking about eco-tourism. For questions 1 – 5, choose from the list **A – H** why each person is speaking. Use the letters only once. There are three extra letters which you do not need to use.

1 Speaker 1 ☐

2 Speaker 2 ☐

3 Speaker 3 ☐

4 Speaker 4 ☐

5 Speaker 5 ☐

A criticising someone else's choice of holiday

B persuading someone to book a particular holiday

C warning someone about what not to do

D admitting he/she was wrong about something

E prohibiting someone from going on holiday

F reporting on alternatives to conventional holidays

G learning about eco-tourism at school

H going on holiday with friends

Exam Reminder

Identifying the function of speech

- Remember to focus on why someone is speaking because that will give you an idea of the purpose.

- Try to concentrate on phrases that express the function rather than on individual words.

- Remember that if you focus on individual words and these appear in the options, you might choose the wrong answer.

C 8.1 ▶️ Listen again and check your answers.

Grammar

Mixed Conditionals

A Look at the picture and complete the sentences using conditionals.

1 If someone hadn't thrown a lighted match, _____.

2 If fire engines don't get here soon, _____.

3 If all the trees are burnt down, _____.

4 If it gets any windier, _____.

5 If there are any animals in the forest, _____.

6 If large amounts of carbon dioxide are emitted into the atmosphere like this, _____.

B Circle the correct words.

1 If we hadn't wasted so much energy, fossil fuels wouldn't / won't be in danger of running out now.
2 Providing governments will give / give subsidies, more people will choose to build eco homes.
3 If we had protected / protect the dodo's natural habitat, would it be extinct now?
4 Supposing there is / was a green society in your town, would you join it?
5 We wouldn't have to deal with a natural disaster if the tanker hadn't / hasn't spilt the oil it was carrying.
6 As long as we all make an effort to consume less, there is / will be a reduction in environmental pollution.
7 If I had been / was quicker in the shower, there would now be hot water left for Dad.
8 Supposing your home was destroyed by a natural disaster, what do / would you do?

Conditionals without *if*

C Complete the sentences with one word. Do not use *if*.

1 I will start a green blog _____ you help to design it.
2 _____ there was a hurricane, would you be frightened?
3 If they hadn't predicted the tsunami, many people _____ be dead now.
4 If the aid agencies _____ arrived on time, we would have fewer casualties.
5 As _____ as you water the plants, I'll mow the lawn.
6 They'll help clean up the beach, _____ condition that the council provide bins.

Use your English

A Complete the sentences with the correct form of the words.

1 Carbon dioxide _____ from cars is a major pollutant.   **EMIT**
2 The faulty solar panel _____ into flames.   **BURST**
3 Wind power is a _____ source of energy.   **RENEW**
4 The hurricane hit _____ regions in the early hours of the morning.   **COAST**
5 During the eclipse, the moon _____ out the sun.   **BLOCK**
6 Due to planting the same crops each year, soil _____ has made the land infertile.   **ERODE**
7 The pond usually _____ over in icy water.   **FREEZE**
8 Photovoltaic or _____ panels use power to generate electricity.   **SUN**

B For questions 1 – 10, read the text below and decide which answer (a, b, c or d) best fits each gap.

Saving the ploughshare tortoise

Since 1986, the Durrell (1) ___ Trust has been working in Madagascar to try to save some of its most vulnerable animals. Among them is the ploughshare tortoise which is on the critically (2) ___ list. These animals used to be (3) ___ from outside dangers in the Baly Bay National Park. But in recent years, the increasing demand for them as pets has become a(n) (4) ___ to their survival. (5) ___ have been entering the park and stealing tortoises so that they can sell them on the black market. Conservationists estimate that only 1000 of these animals exist in the wild and they have gone to unusual lengths to offer them protection (6) ___ theft. In order to (7) ___ people from stealing these beautiful animals, conservationists have begun engraving numbers on their shells. They believe that this makes them less attractive and signals to anyone seeing such an animal outside the park that the animal is stolen. They hope that by signalling that it is (8) ___ the law to trade in these animals, buyers will think twice about purchasing them. By showing buyers that they are participants in a criminal (9) ___, conservationists hope to reduce demand for the tortoises as pets. If they don't succeed, the species will be (10) ___ out in a few years. The Trust, local people and local authorities are working together to ensure that this species survives and that those found guilty of smuggling receive the highest sentences possible.

1	a	Solar	b	Conservation	c	Agriculture	d	Criminal
2	a	endangered	b	consumed	c	extreme	d	biological
3	a	satisfied	b	exposed	c	safe	d	aware
4	a	threat	b	victim	c	effect	d	rise
5	a	Terrorists	b	Robbers	c	Thieves	d	Kidnappers
6	a	from	b	for	c	on	d	with
7	a	object	b	rely	c	discourage	d	search
8	a	under	b	out	c	against	d	away
9	a	case	b	act	c	crime	d	misdemeanour
10	a	wiped	b	blocked	c	burst	d	worn

C Complete the *Exam Task.*

Exam Task

For questions **1 – 10**, read the text below and think of the word which best fits each gap. Use only **one** word in each gap.

On your bike!

Many environmentalists are wondering whether Europe (1) _____ meet its target for reducing carbon emissions. The EU's goal is for 80% to 90% of emissions to (2) _____ reduced by 2050, taking the 1990 levels as a starting point. The European Cycling Federation (ECF), which (3) _____ based in Brussels, think they have a solution that would partly help to get Europe on target. They claim that (4) _____ all European citizens cycled as much as the Danes, it would result (5) _____ greenhouse gases being reduced by around 25%. If more people (6) _____ their bikes instead of using private cars, this figure (7) _____ be even higher. The Danes, it would seem, are very keen (8) _____ cycling. The average Dane cycles 600 miles per year. That's a huge difference between the average for all Europeans, which is less (9) _____ 120 miles per year. What is more, the figures quoted by the ECF don't (10) _____ into consideration the harmful effects building roads, car parks, maintaining and disposing of cars have on the environment. Calculations made by the ECF have shown that only 21 g of emissions are created per cyclist per kilometre, in comparison to 271 g for car passengers and 101 g for bus passengers.

Writing: an essay (2)

A Read the writing task below and write T (true) or F (false).

You have recently had a discussion in your English class about the environment and who is responsible for dealing with pollution. Now your teacher has asked you to write an essay, giving your opinion of the following statement.

> Environmental pollution should be dealt with by governments.

Write your **essay** in 140–190 words in an appropriate style.

1 Your essay must agree with the statement. ☐
2 You should analyse in depth all the consequences of environmental pollution. ☐
3 You should make some reference to the people who are responsible for polluting the environment. ☐
4 You should state your view on the matter in your essay. ☐
5 Your essay will be formal. ☐

Learning Reminder

Avoiding common mistakes
- Always leave yourself enough time to check your essay for mistakes.
- Check all spelling, especially words with double letters, prefixes and suffixes.
- Be careful with words that are easily confused like there, they're and their.
- Make sure you use the correct verb tenses and alway check punctuation, especially apostrophes.

B Read the example essay and complete it with these words and phrases.

> Also   For instance   However   indeed   In fact   Nonetheless   though   To sum up

Without a doubt, environmental pollution causes huge problems worldwide. It is time action was taken to reverse its harmful effects. The question is, **(1)** _____, are only governments responsible for dealing with this issue?

I fully support environmental groups who put pressure on governments to take responsibility for dealing with companies who pollute our air, land and water. Governments **(2)** _____ have an important role to play in making sure that all companies operate according to green policies and enforce penalties on those who break the law.

(3) _____, I strongly disagree that governments, alone should take all the responsibility.

(4) _____, we all have a part to play in ensuring that our world is as clean as possible. **(5)** _____, if we know that a company pollutes the environment, we should stop buying its products. **(6)** _____, we should adopt more environmentally-friendly practices in our everyday lives.

(7) _____, governments must lead the way in creating a greener environment. **(8)** _____, we all must accept responsibility for our environment and strive to make the earth a cleaner place.

C Read and complete the *Exam Task* below. Don't forget to use the *Useful Expressions* on page 105 of your Student's Book.

Exam Task

You have recently had a discussion in your English class about the environment and which issues require greater attention. Now your teacher has asked you to write an essay, giving your opinion of the following statement.

> We must save the giant panda at all costs.

Write your **essay** in 140–190 words in an appropriate style.

↻ Writing Reference p. 185 in Student's Book ▶

Vocabulary

A Choose the correct answers.

1 I can't believe I was taken ___ by that cheat!
a up   c in
b through   d for

2 Two bank employees have been taken ___ in a robbery.
a guilty   c goods
b hostage   d suspect

3 ___ forms of energy like wind and solar power are catching on.
a Fossil   c Renewable
b Greenhouse   d Global

4 The sudden ___ flooded the whole region.
a downpour   c draught
b drought   d gust

5 This charity helps victims ___ natural disasters.
a to   c on
b from   d of

6 Have the jury reached a ___ yet?
a case   c verdict
b sentence   d record

7 Sam has got a ___ record for assault.
a stolen   c life
b hardened   d criminal

8 ___ levels are rising due to global warming.
a Sea   c Rainfall
b Coastal   d Crude

9 The lake ___ because of sub-zero temperatures.
a wore away   c wiped out
b froze over   d blew over

10 Are these crops ___ modified?
a environmentally c genetically
b falsely   d deadly

11 The river ___ was strong and the canoe moved quickly.
a current   c delta
b bank   d cycle

12 Soil ___ is a major agricultural problem here.
a erosion   c deforestation
b emission   d forces

13 Linda can't cope ___ life in prison.
a on   c in
b for   d with

14 Don't be so ___ about the future of the planet!
a pessimistic c aware
b exposed   d keen

15 He ___ to the crime and spent time in prison.
a committed   c accused
b confessed   d pleaded

16 After the tsunami, ___ stole goods from shops.
a blackmailers c hijackers
b muggers   d looters

17 Help! That man has ___ my bag!
a robbed   c burgled
b stolen   d held up

18 The cameraman was hidden ___ sight of the lions.
a to   c from
b out   d under

19 Chemical ___ in food are dangerous to our health.
a organisms   c resources
b fertilisers d gases

20 The police officer was working in ___ clothes.
a plain   c free
b masked   d normal

21 It's ___ the law to break the speed limit.
a against   c versus
b counter   d beside

22 She can see ___ your scheme!
a over   c through
b about   d up

23 You should ___ yourself up to the police.
a hold   c give
b put   d take

24 I think it's time you ___ up to your crimes.
a owned   c gave
b showed   d turned

25 They had an argument, but it had ___ over by the evening.
a blown   c gone
b burst   d flown

26 Let's go skating if the pond is frozen ___.
a out   c over
b hard   d up

27 The woolly mammoth was ___ out during the Ice Age.
a swept   c cleaned
b brushed   d wiped

28 I was talked ___ volunteering by my friends.
a on   c inside
b over   d into

Grammar

B Choose the correct answers.

1 At what time ___?
   a did the suspect arrest
   b had the suspect arrested
   c was the suspect arrested
   d the suspect was arrested

2 Are you ___ solar panels installed?
   a having   c doing
   b being   d putting

3 ___ the weather is good, can we visit the national park?
   a As long   c Unless
   b Supposing   d On condition

4 If I ___ the judge, I'd give a harsher sentence.
   a had been   c were
   b am   d would be

5 If there's an earthquake, people ___ to panic.
   a tend   c would tend
   b will tend   d tended

6 I'll plead guilty on condition that I ___ a reduced sentence.
   a get   c am getting
   b will get   d would get

7 If we ___ onto the roof, we would have drowned.
   a didn't climb   c hadn't climbed
   b don't climb   d won't climb

8 The suspect refused ___ without the presence of a lawyer.
   a question   c to be questioned
   b to question   d questioning

9 Shelley ___ last night.
   a had her car window smashed
   b had smashed her car window
   c her car window had smashed
   d was having her car window smashed

10 Why don't you get a technician ___ the wires?
   a checking   c checked
   b check   d to check

11 If the kidnapper hadn't been caught, Tania ___ missing.
   a is still   c was still
   b would still be   d will still be

12 The prisoners must ___ accompanied at all times.
   a to be   c being
   b been   d be

13 If you ___ anyone, I'll explain the plan to you.
   a don't tell   c aren't telling
   b wouldn't tell   d haven't told

14 If he had been set free earlier, he ___ happier.
   a has been   c would have been
   b will be   d had been

15 I ___ that building on fire if I were you!
   a don't set   c wouldn't have set
   b won't set   d wouldn't set

16 They ___ burgled four times this year.
   a are being   c have been
   b are   d to be

17 Two giant pandas have been ___ to Edinburgh Zoo.
   a send   c to send
   b sending   d sent

18 If it ___ for the storm, we would have arrived hours ago.
   a hadn't been   c wouldn't be
   b wasn't being   d didn't

19 When is the court cased due ___ heard?
   a being   c be
   b to be   d will be

20 Houses ___ up in preparation for the hurricane.
   a boarded   c had boarded
   b were boarded   d were board

21 If I ___ you, I wouldn't do that.
   a were   c be
   b am   d was

22 You will ___ shown to your room now!
   a be   c have
   b being   d having

23 We ___ new doors put in our house.
   a have had   c having
   b have get   d getting

24 ___ it rains tomorrow, what shall we do?
   a Providing   c Thinking
   b Supposing   d Imagining

25 As ___ as you are happy, I am happy too.
   a far   c long
   b tall   d wide

26 I got my sister ___ my homework for me.
   a doing   c do
   b to do   d did

27 She'll do it, on the ___ that you pay her.
   a situation   c provided
   b condition   d promise

Reading

A Read the *Exam Reminder*. How should you deal with this sort of task?

_____

B Now complete the *Exam Task*.

A

Aaron is an author.

"I've always wanted to write. The pleasure I feel from putting myself in someone else's shoes is just immense, and I love creating different worlds away from this dreary two-bedroom house in this busy industrial city. I have been working from home for many years as a freelance writer, and thoroughly enjoy the freedom it gives me. For example, I can choose when to work – personally, my best working times are first thing in the morning and last thing at night. I love the fact that I don't have to commute every day at 7am either. I must admit though that sometimes I wish I had colleagues to bounce ideas off – asking my wife is fine, but sometimes it would be useful to hear a couple of opinions on a new idea."

B

Suzie is a volunteer at an animal shelter.

"I am proud to be able to say that I make a difference in my community by making it safer for animals. I spread the word about being a responsible pet owner, and assist with fundraising events. Walking dogs at the shelter also means I am physically quite fit! The job can sometimes be tough, particularly when I have to be the bearer of bad news if, for example, an animal becomes ill. I feel honoured to be able to help the animals here and dream of working full time in this line of work. There is a new opening for a supervisor at the shelter, and I think I'm going to send in an application!"

C

Sophie is a school teacher.

"I remember being really passionate about my subject at school and my love for the subject is what inspired me to teach it; it just makes me tick. I adore being creative and thinking of new ways to teach the children something. Being a sociable person, I also really enjoy the interaction with children that teaching provides. They can provide such laughs! The main drawback which many teachers find is the work-life balance. Mine isn't too bad, but I do have to work at home quite often – even after the school day has finished."

D

Tom is an office manager.

"My main responsibility is ensuring the business is operating smoothly on a day-to-day basis without any problems. Being a manager means that some of the most important skills to possess are leadership skills. You also need great people skills, as listening, talking and understanding is all crucial. Depending on the day, I will either work in the office or have a meeting with clients. I meet many clients each month, and so have to maintain a neat appearance at all times. My work also involves motivating my team, and I have to do my best so that other people in the office can work efficiently. Ultimately this can mean there is a lot of pressure!"

Exam Task

You are going to read about four people's jobs. For questions **1 – 10**, choose from the paragraphs **A – D**. The paragraphs may be chosen more than once.

Which person / people

1 prides themself on helping the community? ☐
2 does a job which involves working with young people? ☐
3 discusses how important it is to work well with staff? ☐
4 mentions a sad and unpleasant aspect of their job? ☐
5 mentions what they would like to do in the future? ☐
6/7 values their communication skills? ☐ ☐
8 enjoys being free to choose when to work? ☐
9 is conscious of their job affecting their home life? ☐
10 occasionally misses not having a workforce? ☐

Vocabulary

A Complete the words in the sentences.

1 Working for a charity gives me a great sense of s _ _ _ _ _ _ _ _ _ _ _.
2 Factory output is up this month as the staff have been very p _ _ _ _ _ _ _ _ _.
3 At the end of the temporary c _ _ _ _ _ _ _ he was offered a permanent position.
4 There's less job security if you work f _ _ _ _ _ _ _ _.
5 Unfortunately, Brett isn't very p _ _ _ _ _ _ _ and is often late for work.
6 Following her p _ _ _ _ _ _ _ _ to the position of supervisor, Judy seems much happier.
7 What are the w _ _ _ _ _ _ conditions like in your company?
8 I love my job, but my c _ _ _ _ _ _ _ _ _ aren't very friendly.

B Complete the sentences with the correct form of the words.

1 We have three _____ for cashiers at the moment.   OPEN
2 Please report any problems to your _____.   SUPERVISE
3 If you want time off, please ask for _____ a month in advance.   PERMIT
4 Jan has been a flight _____ for five years.   ATTEND
5 Places on the training course are subject to _____.   AVAILABLE
6 Another two _____ are waiting to be interviewed.   APPLY
7 How many _____ are we taking on this year?   EMPLOY
8 Our new business wasn't as _____ as we had expected.   PROFIT

Grammar

Relative Clauses

A Find and correct the mistakes in the sentences. Sometimes more than one answer is possible.

1 Who's the man which Gina is talking to? _____
2 This is the factory that I work. _____
3 The woman who's briefcase was stolen is my boss. _____
4 The desk, which you will be working, used to be mine. _____
5 Speak to the accountant deals with payment of salaries. _____
6 This isn't the application form where you should fill in. _____
7 Do you know who he was made redundant? _____
8 The year which I retire, I'll throw a big party. _____

B Complete the sentences with *who, which, why, where, when, whose, that* or -. Sometimes more than one answer is possible.

1 My supervisor, _____ is very popular with the staff, is being promoted.
2 Is there anyone at work _____ you can confide in?
3 I don't understand _____ you applied for a position so far away.
4 The shop, _____ is closing down soon, is having a huge sale.
5 The cashier put the goods in a bag _____ was torn.
6 The building _____ you work is very beautiful.
7 Does anyone know _____ overalls these are?
8 Easter is _____ we are at our busiest.

Listening

A Read the *Exam Reminder*. What should you do the first time you listen?

_____

B 🔊 **9.1** ▶️ Now listen and complete the *Exam Task*.

Exam Reminder

Using stem questions to find the answer

- Don't forget to look at the questions first. Try to understand what kind of information you will need to answer them.
- The first time you listen, just focus on the question and try to answer it in your own words.
- Then look at the options **a – c** and compare them with your own answer.

Exam Task

You will hear an interview with a student and a careers advisor. For questions 1 – 6, choose the best answer, (**a, b** or **c**).

1 What should students be doing this year according to the speaker?
  a studying for their final exams
  b looking into career choices available to them
  c getting the appropriate qualifications for their chosen job

2 What does the Careers Advice Department offer students access to?
  a the Internet
  b addresses of prospective employers
  c a specialised reference section

3 How can the Careers Advice Department benefit students who have already chosen a career?
  a It can put them in touch with their future employers.
  b It can write letters to employers on their behalf.
  c It can assist them in customising their CV.

4 Why is it important to perform well in job interviews?
  a to stand out among other well-qualified candidates
  b to show that you have gained the necessary qualifications
  c to demonstrate the skills needed for the job

5 What can students do at the workshops run by the Careers Advice Department?
  a give advice to other participants
  b experience a simulated interview
  c put together a professional-looking CV

6 What can you do if you want to attend the forthcoming workshop?
  a check the department website for details
  b turn up at the department's reception on the first day
  c fill in the worksheet the advisor hands out

C 🔊 **9.1** ▶️ Listen again and check your answers.

Grammar

Participle Clauses

A Complete the sentences with the correct participle form of the verbs in brackets.

1 _____ (wait) to be called into the interview room, Tania was very nervous.
2 _____ (disappoint) that he didn't get the job, Brian tore up the letter.
3 _____ (be) in charge of the kindergarten, Ms Dawson felt a great sense of responsibility.
4 _____ (wear) a new suit, the manager looked very smart.
5 Candidates _____ (hand) in their application forms late won't be considered for the post.
6 Employees _____ (train) last month don't have to attend this month's training session.
7 Goods _____ (handle) on this production line meet the highest standards.
8 Drivers _____ (arrive) at the Johnston Road entrance must show ID.

B Circle the correct words.

(1) Worked / Working as a manager in a big company seems like the ideal job to many young people (2) starting / started their careers. (3) Attending / Attended business lunches and (4) travelling / travelled to far off lands for conferences are often perceived to be perks of the manager's job. Often (5) made / making out to be glamorous, managerial positions can in fact be more difficult than they appear. Positions (6) requiring / required managers to take on extra duties such as going to lunches and (7) organised / organising conferences often require that the manager give up a considerable amount of his or her free time. (8) Employed / Employing to do a very responsible job, managers find themselves doing huge amounts of overtime in order to fulfil all their obligations. (9) Taken / Taking on extra responsibility is something that those keen to climb up the career ladder do willingly. A few years down the line, though, it can start to become the source of great stress. (10) Exhausted / Exhausting by years of working late and constant business trips abroad, many managers decide that it's just not worth the hassle. As a result, many give up their white-collar positions for jobs with a lot less responsibility and more reasonable working hours.

Use your English

A For questions 1 – 6, complete the second sentence so that it has a similar meaning to the first sentence, using the word given. Do not change the word given. You must use between two and five words including the word given.

1 I met my wife in this place.
   where
   This_____
   I met my wife.

2 That girl's father is in prison.
   whose
   That's_____
   is in prison.

3 We ate a delicious meal last night.
   that
   The meal _____
   was delicious.

4 I got a new laptop for my last birthday.
   when
   My last birthday _____
   I got a new laptop.

5 He lost because he didn't train hard enough.
   why
   Not training hard enough _____
   he lost.

6 The kidnapper escaped last week, but was arrested again yesterday.
   who
   Yesterday they arrested _____
   last week.

B For questions 1 – 12, read the text below and decide which answer (a, b, c, or d) best fits each gap.

Directors wanted for summer schools

Are you an experienced TEFL teacher with management experience looking for a(n) (1) _____ way to spend next summer? If you raised your (2) _____, then maybe you should consider applying for one of the four (3) _____ in the directors' department available with Contact English Schools this summer. At Contact, we have a truly international feel with students coming from 30 countries worldwide. All with one aim: to (4) _____ their English. If you're looking for extra responsibility and would enjoy the challenge of having up to 30 (5) _____ under you, then this job will (6) _____ you down to the ground. During the courses, (7) _____ are run in some of the most prestigious boarding schools in the country, students sleep in dormitories. Staff are offered free accommodation in the schools' teaching accommodation wings. Although you won't (8) _____ rich in the four weeks you will be working at the summer school, you will be (9) _____ with the highest salary available for such a position: £900 per week. All employees are entitled to take one day (10) _____ per week. (11) _____ online at www.contactenglish.co.uk. Please note, only candidates (12) _____ have a degree in teaching English and previous management experience will be called for an interview.

	a		b		c		d
1	a individual	b	independent	c	reliable	d	profitable
2	a mark	b	hand	c	fees	d	brains
3	a openings	b	shifts	c	promotions	d	supervisors
4	a request	b	improve	c	involve	d	commute
5	a attendants	b	companions	c	coaches	d	teachers
6	a match	b	dismiss	c	suit	d	fill
7	a that	b	which	c	where	d	-
8	a get	b	make	c	take	d	put
9	a monitored	b	supported	c	returned	d	rewarded
10	a out	b	on	c	over	d	off
11	a Request	b	Apply	c	Attend	d	Hire
12	a what	b	whose	c	who	d	when

C Complete the *Exam Task* below.

Exam Task

For questions **1 – 10**, read the text below. Use the word given in capitals at the end of some of the lines to form a word that fits in the gap **in the same line**.

Dress for Success

In the jobs market, it's not enough to have experience, qualifications and (1) _____   **AVAILABLE**
to work shifts and weekends. Competition is so fierce that hundreds of (2) _____ may   **APPLY**
send in their CVs for just one job. This may sound (3) _____, but for the majority of   **DEPRESS**
unemployed women, it's an unfortunate reality. After years of unemployment, many people become
(4) _____ and begin to lose hope as well as their self-confidence.   **SATISFY**

There are many unemployed people in the UK. We have discovered a new charity, called Dress
for Success, which focuses particularly on unemployment among women. To make sure they
dress (5) _____ for interviews, this charity provides women with interview clothes   **SUITABLE**
and a handbag. This makes them more confident when applying for (6) _____   **VACANT**
and gives them a more positive attitude, as they might worry they don't (7) _____   **POSSESS**
an appropriate smart outfit. The charity has also received (8) _____ from large   **PERMIT**
companies to arrange meetings between their (9) _____ and unemployed women.   **EMPLOY**
This gives the women the chance to ask these workers about conditions in their jobs and gives
them the (10) _____ of knowing that they aren't so different from women in   **SATISFY**
employment. The charity hopes that these initiatives will help boost these women's self-image when
attending interviews so that they will be more successful in securing a job.

Writing: a formal letter (2)

A Read the writing task below and answer the questions.

You have seen the following job advertisement in your local newspaper.

School bus driver wanted for Kidzone Kindergarten

Kidzone is a family run kindergarten for pre-school children. We currently have a vacancy for a driver to take young children to and from school. A clean driving licence is essential. Previous experience is not necessary, but the successful candidate must have the right personality for working with under sixes. Please apply in writing to the kindergarten principal, Ms Jean Broody, saying why you are suitable for the job.

Write your **letter** in 140–190 words in an appropriate style.

1 What are you asked to write?
2 What job is advertised?
3 What does the job involve?
4 What kind of qualifications would the ideal candidate have?
5 What kind of personality would be suitable for this job?

B Read the model letter and fill in the interview form below for the candidate based on the information in the letter.

Dear Ms Broody,

I am writing in order to apply for the position of school bus driver, which I saw advertised in the *Bradford Times*.

I am thirty years old and I have been driving for ten years. In 2005, I gained my professional driving licence and I have worked as a taxi driver and as a mini-bus driver for a holiday company. My driving licence is clean and I have never had any accidents.

In my previous job as a mini-bus driver, I had the opportunity to work with children. This experience taught me how important road safety is when dealing with young passengers.

I am hard working, honest and punctual. Also, I have a friendly personality and get on particularly well with young children. For these reasons, I believe I am a suitable candidate for the position.

I look forward to your reply.

Yours faithfully,

Stirling Moss

Interview form

Position: School bus driver
Applicant's name: (1) _____
Applicant's age: (2) _____
Relevant qualifications: (3) _____
_____
_____

Previous experience: (4) _____
_____
_____

Experience with children: (5) Yes ☐ No ☐
Character: (6) _____
_____
_____

Interview: 3.30 pm, Thursday 5th May
To be interviewed by: Jean Broody

C Read and complete the *Exam Task* below. Don't forget to use the *Useful Expressions* on page 119 of your Student's Book.

Exam Task

You have seen the following job advertisement in your local newspaper.

Dog walkers needed at Huntingfield Kennels

Are you an animal-lover who is available early mornings and late in the evenings seven days a week? Do you love spending time with dogs? If so, then we may have the perfect job for you. We require two dog walkers in the Huntingfield area to exercise our dogs on a regular basis. Only those with previous experience will be considered for the position. Apply in writing to the kennel manager explaining why you are suitable for the job.

Write your **letter** in 140–190 words in an appropriate style.

Reading

A Read the *Exam Reminder*. What should you remember about the answers?

_____

B Now complete the *Exam Task*.

Outdoor Kindergartens

An alternative choice for the blooming generation!

Norway is one of the most sophisticated and modern countries in the world, yet more and more Norwegian parents are going back to nature when it comes to raising their offspring. Thanks to Norway's Outdoor Kindergartens, working mums and dads now have the option of having their children looked after in the great outdoors.

The north of Norway falls inside the Arctic Circle, which means the country is in darkness for two months a year and winter temperatures often fall below zero. In spite of the tough climate, there are hundreds of Outdoor Kindergartens all over the country. These kindergartens have the same content and tasks as Norway's conventional kindergartens, but their teaching
line 13 methods vary greatly.

Set on the sea shore at the foot of a fjord, Tusseladden Outdoor Kindergarten is surrounded by the most beautiful landscape imaginable. Heidi Burang is an outdoor group leader at this school. She claims that in a world where children are bombarded with computers and electronic games, it's essential to motivate children to want to go outdoors. It's just as important, however, to occupy them creatively once they are out, she says. Motivation has a huge role to play in the education of all children, even more so when children face difficult circumstances. As a result, group leaders like Heidi encourage children to explore nature and their own boundaries, rather than spending most of the day imposing boundaries on them.

At most kindergartens, children are brought inside when it rains or if it's cold. Not in Tusseladden. Norwegians have a saying, 'There's no such thing as bad weather, just bad clothes.' Children at outdoor kindergartens arrive in the morning dressed in several layers of warm clothing with a waterproof all-in-one on top, Wellington boots, a hat and gloves. They are all set for a day in nature, even in the lowest of temperatures. If the Kindergarten Act states that they have to make certain constructions, for example a boat, these youngsters head for the shore. In most countries, this kind of construction would be made with material specially designed for children in a controlled environment. At Tusseladden the children are introduced to real tools such as hammers and saws and, with the assistance of the group leader, use these tools to construct their very own boats using driftwood found along the shore. Once they are ready, their boats are launched into the water to test how well they float. Heidi Burang says that being outdoors for this kind of activity has the advantage of allowing children, who live in the 'here and now', to try and test things immediately.

Outdoors they can even dig up potatoes in the school garden for their lunch. This is more than just a fun activity to reward them as the group leader can exploit it to teach them about shapes, numbers, cultivating without pesticides and about how previous generations cultivated crops. Having dug up potatoes, the children – with the help and close supervision of a group leader – light a fire outdoors in order to cook them for lunch. This may seem like an extremely dangerous, if not irresponsible, thing to allow a five year old to do. Heidi, however, has a different perspective. She explains that danger is all around us. We can't escape it so we should help children to manage risk and not try to eliminate it.

When most parents ask their preschoolers 'What did you do at school today?', they don't expect to be told that their child hiked to the peak of a 500 m mountain. Yet this is exactly what the older children at Tusseladden Outdoor Kindergarten embarked on today. Through rain and a cold north wind, these incredible youngsters made it to the top whilst mastering invaluable skills for life such as perseverance, orientation, being adaptable, looking after their own rucksack and helping out others. An added bonus is that walking on uneven terrain, like the surface of the mountain they climbed, helps to improve their motor skills.

Norwegian children are born into one of the world's wealthiest countries. With the help of outdoor kindergartens, they are shown from a very early age that the most valuable things in life are found in nature.

You are going to read an article about Outdoor Kindergartens in Norway. For questions **1 – 8**, choose the answer (**a, b, c** or **d**) which you think fits best according to the text.

1 Norwegian parents have the choice to
  a have their children attend the most sophisticated and modern schools in the world.
  b send their preschoolers to schools which work outside.
  c set up Outdoor Kindergartens.
  d take their children to work with them.

2 What does *their* in line 13 refer to?
  a conventional kindergartens
  b kindergarten content and tasks
  c Outdoor Kindergartens
  d winter temperatures

3 Tusseladden Outdoor Kindergarten is
  a in a remarkable location.
  b the only one of its kind.
  c owned by Heidi Burang.
  d at the peak of a fjord.

4 Heidi Burang expresses concern about
  a the extremely difficult circumstances children at the school face.
  b the negative effect technology has on today's children.
  c children who only want to play outdoors.
  d how to find ways to motivate children.

5 Why does the writer quote a Norwegian saying in paragraph 4?
  a to show that if we are properly dressed, we can go out despite bad weather
  b to comment on how badly Norwegians dress
  c to suggest that Norwegians don't understand how bad Norwegian weather is
  d to say that the children at the kindergarten wear too many clothes

6 What aspect of Tusseladden Outdoor Kindergarten is similar to other Norwegian kindergartens?
  a the materials children use
  b the learning environment
  c the teaching methods used
  d the tasks children are given

7 What does the description of children lighting a fire tell us?
  a that every school has its troublemakers
  b that children can be shown how to deal with danger
  c that the children were extremely hungry
  d that the school isn't well equipped

8 According to the writer, mountain climbing can teach children
  a to count.
  b to recognise shapes.
  c to be responsible.
  d to appreciate old methods of growing crops.

Vocabulary

A Match the first half of the sentences (1 – 6) to the second half (a – f).

1 Helen has just enrolled ☐
2 Don't forget to raise ☐
3 Some students have to repeat ☐
4 I wish our teacher wouldn't give ☐
5 I'm going to have to retake ☐
6 My sister got ☐

  a your hand if you need help.
  b the biology exam I failed.
  c into university last year.
  d on a cookery course.
  e us so much homework at the weekend!
  f a year at school after a serious illness.

B Complete the words in the sentences.

1 I have a private t _ _ _ _ for Italian.
2 Brian won a s _ _ _ _ _ _ _ _ _ _ to pay his college fees.
3 Who won the tennis t _ _ _ _ _ _ _ _ ?
4 We had to wear long black gowns at g _ _ _ _ _ _ _ _ .
5 C _ _ _ _ _ _ _ in exams is completely unacceptable.
6 Don's missed a lot of classes, so he will find this a _ _ _ _ _ _ _ _ _ difficult.
7 The teacher's lack of d _ _ _ _ _ _ _ _ meant that the pupils were very noisy in class.
8 Some boarding schools have very expensive f _ _ _ .

Grammar

Reported Speech

A Complete the second sentences so that they have a similar meaning to the first sentences using the words in bold. Use between two and five words.

1 'Cheating won't help you in the long run,' said Ms Fuddy.

me

Ms Fuddy said that _____ in the long run.

2 'You have been absent too often this term,' the head teacher said.

I

The head teacher said that _____ too often that term.

3 'Hand in your homework on time!' the teacher said to me.

to

The teacher told _____ homework on time.

4 'Can I sit beside you in chemistry?' Clarissa asked.

she

Clarissa asked me _____ beside me in chemistry.

5 'The teacher gave us too much homework yesterday,' said Lana.

given

Lana said that _____ too much homework the previous day.

6 'Put your bags here,' the coach said.

our

The coach told us _____.

B Circle the correct words.

1 Mary asked if Joe wants / does Joe want to apply for the course.
2 He asked me when I graduated / had graduated.
3 The librarian told to me / me I couldn't take ten books out at one time.
4 The students said they will have / had to complete the assignment by the following day.
5 The careers counsellor said / told us to drop by whenever we were free.
6 Fran said she had been absent only once the last / previous year.
7 The head teacher told us don't / not to run in the corridor.
8 Mum said I would / will pass my exams if I studied.

Listening

A Read the *Exam Reminder*. How many words should your answers have?

_____

B [10.1 ▶] Listen and complete the *Exam Task*.

Exam Reminder

Completing sentences

- Remember that in these types of task, you should write between one and three words for each question.
- Before you listen for a second time, check your answers don't have more than three words.
- When checking your answers, check that they all make sense grammatically and don't repeat information before or after the gaps.

Exam Task

You will hear a TV broadcast with a teenager. For questions **1 – 10**, complete the sentences with a word or short phrase.

1 There are 42 _____ in Greece according to the presenter.
2 The Pallini school has been operating since _____.
3 Currently, _____ students attend Hara's school.
4 Hara and her classmates must study _____ such as maths as well as music.
5 The music lessons consist of music _____ plus playing instruments.
6 Hara will take her violin exams _____.
7 Hara and her friends send each other _____ that they make.
8 Annita is the _____ of Hara's band.
9 The _____ at school sometimes helps the band with song lyrics.
10 Hara says they'll have limited time for _____ for School Wave due to exams.

C [10.1 ▶] Listen again and check your answers.

Grammar

Reporting Verbs

A Change the direct speech into reported speech using these verbs in the correct form.

admit   advise   agree   apologise   deny   offer   refuse   remind

1 'I won't help you with your homework,' said my sister.
My sister _____.

2 'Yes, I will let you do the experiment in the lab,' said the science teacher.
The science teacher _____.

3 'I didn't cheat in the exam!' said Mary.
Mary _____.

4 'Don't forget to enrol on the course in time,' Dad told me.
Dad _____.

5 'I'm so sorry for spilling coffee on your notebook,' said Virginia.
Virginia _____.

6 'I can teach your son English free of charge,' said Susan.
Susan _____.

7 'You should revise regularly,' the teacher told us.
The teacher _____.

8 'I stole your research,' said Brian's chemistry tutor.
Brian's chemistry tutor _____.

B Find and circle eight mistakes in the text.

National plant a tree week

Schools throughout the UK are busy preparing for National Tree Week. From 26th November to 4th December all schools in the UK are encouraged to plant trees on their school grounds. Head teacher at a primary school in Devon, Isa Green, has decided giving children at her school a break from ordinary lessons in order to plant elm trees at the school entrance. She agreed for plant these trees when she heard about the project, which is run by The Tree Council. She explained to the trees are provided by The Woodland Trust, a national charity. She persuaded all classroom teachers at the school getting involved. She also advised to make use of the 70-page activity booklet issued free to schools by The Woodland Trust to help them prepare for the event. She encouraged them about using activities such as building sculptures out of pine cones, leaves and other materials that students could collect from a nearby forest. At first, some teachers were worried that students might destroy the trees. Green, however, warned students about not to harm the trees. She even announced to students would be severely punished if they did.

Use your English

A For questions 1 – 12, read the text below and think of the word which best fits each gap. Use only one word in each gap.

Jobs for the boys

A French court has found France's former president Jacques Chirac guilty (**1**) _____ corruption. The former president, (**2**) _____ did not attend court to hear the verdict due to ill-health, was given a 14-month suspended sentence. The trial took place in Paris, the city (**3**) _____ Chirac was mayor from 1977 to 1995 – 1995 being the year (**4**) _____ he became president. Chirac was convicted of corruption as he had paid members of his 'Rally for the Republic' party by employing them to do public-service jobs when (**5**) _____ actual position existed. In doing so, he not only spent public money inappropriately, but he also let down the people of Paris and destroyed (**6**) _____ confidence in authority. Chirac is the first former French head of state to be convicted (**7**) _____ 1945. In that year, Marshal Philippe Petain was convicted of collaborating with (**8**) _____ Nazis. Chirac, (**9**) _____ presidency lasted 12 years, was absent from the trial as he is reported to be suffering (**10**) _____ memory loss. (**11**) _____ his conviction represents a victory for the judicial system, it leaves us wondering about (**12**) _____ his sentence was so lenient. Prior to the verdict, he had been expected to face up to 10 years in jail and fines of up to 150,000 euros.

B Now complete the *Exam Task*.

Exam Task

For questions **1 – 8**, complete the second sentence so that it has a similar meaning to the first sentence, using the word given. **Do not change the word given**. You must use between two and five words, including the word given.

1 'I'll give you more homework unless you settle down!' the teacher told us.
warned
The teacher ______________________ give us more homework unless we settled down.

2 Marc Jennings has been at this school for a year and his dad is our maths teacher.
whose
Marc Jennings, ______________________ our maths teacher, has been at this school for a year.

3 'Can I see your article now?' the editor asked the journalist.
she
The editor asked the journalist ______________________ his article at that moment.

4 Shelley told me she didn't apply for the job because the salary was too low.
reason
The ______________________ apply for the job was because the salary was too low.

5 It was my careers counsellor that encouraged me to study fabrics.
person
My careers counsellor ______________________ encouraged me to study fabrics.

6 'You should turn up for work on time,' my supervisor advised me.
punctual
My supervisor ______________________ for work.

7 The woman dressed in green is the company owner.
is
The company owner is ______________________ in green.

8 'Why don't we play football at break?' said Ralph.
playing
Ralph ______________________ football at break.

Learning Reminder

Understanding different functions

- When writing a formal letter or email in response to one you have received, you must address all questions asked and all points raised. You need to understand the different functions of writing (e.g. to describe, explain, suggest, thank, advise, apologise, etc.) and deal with them appropriately.
- Don't forget to use the correct tone when writing. Remember to also use long forms instead of contracted forms; use more formal language; and begin and end your email appropriately.

Writing: a formal email

A Read the writing task and then tick the things you have to do.

You run an English-language summer school. You have just received this email from Mario Barla, a foreign student who is interested in enrolling on a course this summer. Read Mr Barla's email and the notes you have made. Then write an email to Mr Barla using all the notes you have made.

mailbox Today | Mail | Calendar | Contacts

Reply | Reply All | Forward | Delete

From: Mario Barla **Date:** 2nd May **Subject:** Summer courses

I have heard that your summer school has a very good reputation and I am interested in enrolling on a course this summer. → Thank him

I would like to know the dates for intermediate courses in July and would also like to know how much the courses cost. → Tell him

Also, I understand that students at the school must find their own accommodation. Could you tell me if there is suitable accommodation for rent nearby? → Suggest

If there is anything you would like to know about me, please don't hesitate to ask. → Ask him

Yours sincerely,
Mario Barla

Write your **email** in 140–190 words in an appropriate style.

1 Write an informal email to another student. ☐
2 Use all your notes in an appropriate way. ☐
3 Apologise for not replying earlier. ☐
4 Inform the reader about where he could stay. ☐
5 Ask the reader about his level of English. ☐
6 Complain to the reader for not giving enough information about himself. ☐
7 Thank the reader for showing interest in the school. ☐
8 Offer to find accommodation for the reader. ☐

B Read the model email and complete it with these sentences.

a Could you let me know how many years you have been studying English?

b Regarding accommodation, the student halls of residence at the nearby university are usually our students' preferred choice.

c Thank you very much for showing interest in courses at our summer school.

d The fees for both courses are £450, which covers the cost of all materials and two excursions.

e The first course will run from 2nd – 17th July and the second course from 18th – 31st July.

---

mailbox

Reply | Reply All | Forward | Delete

From: Rory Simpson   **Date:** 3rd May   **Subject:** Re: Summer courses

Dear Mr Barla,

(1) _____ It is very encouraging to learn that we have gained a good reputation with previous students.

In your email, you ask for information about intermediate courses in July. We intend to run two courses this year at all levels. (2) _____ Please inform us as soon as possible if you would be interested in the second course as places are limited. (3) _____

(4) _____ They are within walking distance of our classrooms and are reasonably priced.

Finally, in your email you say you are interested in intermediate-level courses. (5) _____

Best wishes,

Rory Simpson

C Read and complete the *Exam Task* below. Don't forget to use the *Useful Expressions* on page 131 of your Student's Book.

Exam Task

You are a teacher at a primary school. You have just received this email from Anna Winters, a local businesswoman and former pupil of the school. Read Ms Winter's email and the notes you have made. Then write an email to Ms Winters using all the notes you have made.

---

mailbox

Today | Mail | Calendar | Contacts

Reply | Reply All | Forward | Delete

From: Anna Winters   **Date:** 19th August   **Subject:** Computers for the school

I am the owner of InfoTech, a successful IT company. As a previous pupil of Dunceton Primary, I would like to make a donation of several computers and tablets to the school. → *Thank her*

As I would like to give one computer and one tablet to each class, could you tell me how many you would like me to send? → *Tell her*

Also, I would like to know when would be the best time for these to be delivered and installed. → *Suggest*

Finally, would it be possible for my staff and I to give talks to the students on the importance of using technology properly? → *Apologise*

Yours sincerely,

Anna Winters

Write your **email** in 140–190 words in an appropriate style.

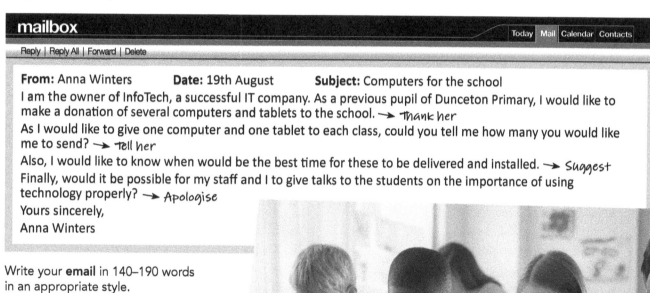

↻ Writing Reference p. 179 in Student's Book

Review 5 — Units 9 & 10

Vocabulary

A Choose the correct answers.

1 Do the employees ___ the initiative in your company?

a make c have

b get d take

2 Marion was caught ___ in the exam.

a rewriting c cheating

b retaking d stealing

3 Luckily, it had been a ___ year for the company.

a reliable c promotional

b profitable d punctual

4 My boss told me to ___ up the good work.

a look c move

b put d keep

5 Boarding school pupils sleep in ___.

a tournaments c scholarships

b dormitories d schedules

6 I'm sure you'll breeze ___ the interview.

a through c in

b across d up

7 Which year did you ___ into university?

a pass c get

b fill d take

8 You must have ___ from your parents to go on the trip.

a licence c commission

b form d permission

9 Speak to the ___ if you want to join the team.

a coach c colleague

b member d counsellor

10 I'm ___ a geography exam tomorrow.

a giving c earning

b sitting d keeping

11 Have you ___ time off this summer?

a applied c requested

b given d hired

12 Sorry, but we don't have any ___ at the moment.

a posts c availability

b absences d openings

13 Workers who are highly ___ will be given a pay rise.

a productive c depressed

b redundant d individual

14 I racked my ___ to find the answer to the problem.

a notes c homework

b brains d brainwave

15 Billy ___ 50 kilometres and back to work every day.

a computes c grasps

b involves d commutes

16 What's your greatest ___ so far this term?

a satisfaction c discipline

b achievement d attendance

17 If you're starting your own business, don't expect to make a ___ immediately.

a profit c rise

b sack d statement

18 I have a private ___ who teaches me Chinese.

a apprentice c attendant

b trainer d tutor

19 Mum's decided to ___ on a carpentry course.

a retire c sign

b dismiss d enrol

20 Why did Martin drop ___ of college?

a out c off

b over d down

21 Could you ___ in this application form, please?

a put c hold

b fill d write

22 She ___ through her final exams easily.

a blew c breezed

b ran d whistled

23 Have you ___ out how to do it yet?

a numbered c calculated

b wondered d figured

24 I'll pop ___ to your house this evening.

a after c through

b under d over

25 Keep ___ the good work, Jerry!

a up c on

b down d off

26 I'm amazed at how quickly you ___ up the language.

a lifted c took

b got d picked

27 Look ___ for the traffic wardens around here!

a out c over

b up d along

28 Oh no! We've run ___ of milk.

a out c over

b off d on

Grammar

B **Choose the correct answers.**

1 Sarah asked if she ___ the following week off.
  a could take   **c** takes
  b ought take   **d** will take

2 The teacher told us ___.
  a we sit down   **c** to sit down
  b sit down   **d** for sitting down

3 That's the office ___ I used to work.
  a that   **c** when
  b which   **d** where

4 Do you know ___ desk this is?
  a who's   **c** -
  b whose   **d** that

5 Employees ___ on in June will be paid in July.
  a taking   **c** who are taking
  b who took   **d** taken

6 The accountant ___ to give me the report.
  a refused   **c** complained
  b denied   **d** admitted

7 The chef, ___ is a friend of mine, is excellent.
  a that   **c** whose
  b who   **d** -

8 Jane told me she ___ her new job soon.
  a had started   **c** was starting
  b will start   **d** started

9 At the interview, they asked me ___ I was married.
  a that   **c** whose
  b whether   **d** who

10 The teacher ___ that make-up is banned at school.
  a said   **c** asked
  b told   **d** wondered

11 The bag ___ me isn't mine.
  a where you gave   **c** whose you gave
  b you gave   **d** who you gave

12 ___ the door, the boy refused to move.
  a Blocked   **c** Blocking
  b Being blocked   **d** Block

13 The counsellor advised ___ for the course.
  a for to sign up   **c** signing up
  b sign up   **d** me to sign up

14 The teacher ___ son I know is very nice.
  a who   **c** whose
  b that   **d** which

15 He'll never forget the day ___ he got the sack.
  a when   **c** which
  b where   **d** whose

16 They said that they had had four tests the ___.
  a last week   **c** next week
  b week before   **d** week previous

17 Our teacher said we were the best class she ___.
  a was taught   **c** had ever taught
  b has ever taught **d** was ever teaching

18 The student behind me asked if ___ my pen.
  a she could borrow   **c** whether she could borrow
  b could she borrow   **d** can she borrow

19 ___ by all his referees, he got the job.
  a Recommending   **c** Recommended
  b To be recommended **d** He was recommended

20 The secretary ___ is over there.
  a ,which they hired,   **c** ,that they hired,
  b they hired   **d** whose they hired

21 Mrs Smith, ___ I thought was on holiday, is here.
  a which   **c** who
  b that   **d** she

22 He apologised ___ being late.
  a for   **c** of
  b to   **d** with

23 The policeman ___ ride on the pavement.
  a told me to not   **c** said me not to
  b told me not to   **d** said me to not

24 ___ being able to dance, I don't enjoy parties.
  a No   **c** Not
  b None   **d** Can't

25 Not wanting ___ rude, I sat quietly until the end of the meal
  a being   **c** was
  b be   **d** to be

26 Do you know the reason ___ it happened?
  a how   **c** which
  b when   **d** why

27 'Where's Greta?'   She decided ___ at home.
  a stay   **c** stayed
  b staying   **d** to stay

28 'Why didn't Dan want to eat anything?' 'He said he ___ dinner.'
  a already has   **c** has already has
  b had already   **d** had already had

Reading

A Read the *Exam Reminder*. What should you do when you don't know what a word or phrase means in a question?

_____

B Now complete the *Exam Task*.

Waking up my senses on a year-long trip!

After finishing school last summer, I decided that I wanted to broaden my horizons. I wanted to see the sights. And I certainly wanted to experience new cultures. With a little persuasion, I convinced my parents to see me off on a year-long adventure…

My first destination was Tuscany – the jewel in the Italian culinary crown! Whilst planning my itinerary before leaving home, my parents told me that Villa Rustica was a must for would-be chefs. And

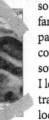

so it was that I made for the most luxurious farmhouse I have ever stayed in, where I participated in a hands-on gourmet cookery course with resident chef Roberto di Caldo and sous-chef Giovanni Pronti. Over the four classes, I learnt how to cook and prepare authentic, traditional, Tuscan dishes using the finest, fresh, local ingredients. As a souvenir I took away a notebook I'd filled during the week with recipes and tips I learnt from the chefs. I'm sure I'll use it all the time when I'm back home! The surroundings were just superb and the Tuscan countryside was absolutely breathtaking! We even got to have a tour of the local vineyards, orchards and olive groves and so I was able to see first hand how the staples of the Italian diet are produced.

A few pounds heavier and with a very full stomach, I set off to France and arrived in the Cote d'Azur in June. The journey was rather distressing (I lost my smart phone and was stopped at customs), but I came up smelling of roses! Whilst on board my plane, I was looking at a travel brochure when I saw an advert saying, "Learn how to beat stars like J-Lo and David Beckham at their own game on a one-, two- or three-day perfume course." Arriving in France, I called the company up and booked in – of course I wanted to create my very own signature scent! I took the longest course and it included an introduction to aromatherapy and essential oils; I discovered how these oils can affect your mood and how to use them to your advantage. There were over 130 different essences to choose from, and we were asked to make the unique aroma that reflects the true you. I even received a personal perfume making assessment from a professional perfume-maker. But even better than that, I registered my formula so that I can put in future orders of my signature scent! The classes ran in the mornings only, leaving me plenty of time to explore the surrounding area and monuments at my leisure.

Then I made for Musical Morocco. I had heard a lot about the Atlas Mountains in the Moroccan desert from talking to a travel agent before I set off, and he said they have gained popularity in recent years with hikers and trekkers in particular. I admitted my sister is better at hiking than I am, but then the travel agent suggested that those who are

more musically inclined will also find a place for themselves in these ancient lands. So I checked in to this guest house in Ouarzazate: a drummer's paradise. Music in this region, like most other aspects of local tradition, is passed down from generation to generation. In keeping with this custom, Abdullaye – a local musician – offers 10-day percussion courses. I just had to book on! Local instruments, such as the djembe, formed the basis of the workshop. But there were also a couple of teenagers who were experienced bongo players, and they brought their instruments along with them for this special free-style evening drum session under the desert sky. It was utterly incredible!

My final stop… well, I'll see if you can guess where I went! I've always fancied myself as an artist, but I've never had any formal art tuition other than lessons at school. So I looked into a painting course at my final destination. I looked online, and when I saw an offer where I could take advantage of the guides to go on safaris and visits to elephant reserves for next to nothing, I immediately enrolled! And so at the end of my adventures in Morocco, off I travelled to… yep, you've guessed it! India. Kerala was my final stop, where I spent ten days in September. During the course, I developed skills and techniques such as learning about basic colours, creating artwork using watercolours, pencil and charcoal, appreciating works of art and a variety of painting and drawing techniques. Each day, top tutors inspired me to create by introducing us to a new theme or exercise. One day we even went on a cruise down Kerala's wonderful waterways. The beauty of this course was that it took place in stunning mountain surroundings away from the busy tourist resorts, so I could mingle with the locals and sample delicious traditional Kerala cuisine. Well, I've now left Kerala and am sat in the departure lounge ready to set off back home. Already, my trip seems a distant memory… but I will never forget it. The more I've travelled, the more I've learnt about different cultures – it's been the trip of a lifetime!

You are going to read a blog about someone's travelling experience. For questions **1 – 5**, choose the answer (**a, b, c** or **d**) which you think fits best according to the text.

1 What was the writer's opinion on the cookery lessons?
  a She didn't think the dishes selected were appropriate choices.
  b They were the least interesting part of the week.
  c She enjoyed them a little.
  d They were extremely valuable and she will put into practice what she learnt when back home.

2 How long was the perfume course the writer participated in?
  a one day
  b two days
  c three days
  d a week

3 What do we discover about the writer in her account of Morocco?
  a She is an experienced bono player.
  b She is very musical.
  c She enjoys hiking.
  d She had already been to the Atlas Mountains.

4 In which country did she travel along rivers?
  a India
  b France
  c Morocco
  d Italy

5 At what point in time is the traveller writing this blog?
  a at the beginning of the trip
  b during her final visit
  c being back home already
  d at the very end of the trip

Vocabulary

A Circle the odd one out.

1	runway	departure lounge	retreat
2	vessel	port	bay
3	overseas	foreign	yacht
4	lagoon	itinerary	gulf
5	international	isolated	remote
6	customs	coves	duty-free shops

B Complete the text by writing one word in each gap.

In the past, going on holiday was simple. You'd go to your local travel (**1**) _____ and pick out the most attractive package (**2**) _____ you could afford. You would book in (**3**) _____ so that you could be super-organised for your holiday. The big day would arrive and before you knew it, you would have your boarding (**4**) _____ in hand and be heading for the (**5**) _____ gate where the aircraft would be waiting outside. Nowadays, however, most people book their holidays online at the last minute. When online booking first came on the scene, some people were a bit suspicious, while others raved at the reduced ticket prices and how easy it was to make a (**6**) _____ at the touch of a button. Cut-price (**7**) _____ fares soon brought problems to the industry, though. Many popular (**8**) _____, who flew holidaymakers to all corners of the globe, found themselves in trouble as a result. These companies soon realised that if a flight wasn't full, they couldn't afford to fly. This often led to flights being cancelled and customers being left stranded. As a result, the days of relaxing holidays seem far back in the past.

Grammar

Comparison of Adjectives & Adverbs

A Complete the sentences with the correct comparative or superlative form of the word given.

1 Hartsfield-Jackson Airport in Atlanta is _____ airport in the world. (busy)

2 Majorca is _____ than Menorca. (popular)

3 Is bungee jumping as _____ as people say it is? (dangerous)

4 It's _____ for me to speak Spanish than Italian. (easy)

5 What is _____ way to get to Tipperary? (good)

6 Let's book our holiday _____ this year than we did last year. (early)

7 The final day of our holiday was _____ of all. (interesting)

8 That was _____ holiday I've ever been on! (bad)

B Complete the sentences by writing one word in each gap.

1 Argos is one of _____ hottest places in Greece.

2 The service is slower in the restaurant _____ in the café.

3 Is Heathrow as convenient for you _____ Gatwick?

4 The more I waited at the departure gate, the _____ impatient I became.

5 The food was _____ bad we couldn't eat it.

6 I only paid £30 to come by bus – that's much _____ than the train, which costs £60.

7 I've had _____ a wonderful holiday!

8 This beach is _____ crowded; let's go to another one.

Listening

A Read the *Exam Reminder*. What should you be careful with?

_____

B 🔊 11.1 ▶ Now complete the *Exam Task*.

Exam Task

You will hear part of a television programme about holidays in Britain. For questions **1 – 7**, choose the best answer (**a, b** or **c**).

1 The holidays on this week's *Globetrotter* will appeal to people who
   a are fairly concerned about travelling by plane.
   b love travelling to international destinations.
   c are utterly frightened at the thought of travelling by plane.

2 Woodland is recommended for those who would like to go to
   a Miami.
   b Mongolia.
   c China.

3 Teepees make an excellent choice of accommodation for
   a extremely experienced campers.
   b families with little camping experience.
   c campers with pets.

4 What can you see from the St Moritz Hotel?
   a South Beach, Miami
   b the Cowshed Spa
   c Daymer Bay

5 The presenter says Chinatown is found in
   a London's Soho district
   b Cornwall
   c Shanghai

6 What can you see in Chinatown during the Chinese New Year?
   a dance performances by a theatre group from Taiwan
   b Asian art exhibitions
   c street parades with Chinese dragons

7 When can you NOT book a self-catering cottage in Portmeirion?
   a from January to March
   b from April to November
   c from 25th December to 1st January

C 🔊 11.1 ▶ Listen again and check your answers.

Grammar

Adjectives & Adverbs

A Choose the correct answers.

1 Visiting Niagara Falls was ___ amazing!

   a extremely   **b** absolutely   **c** slightly

2 I'm ___ worried about flying for the first time.

   a rather   **b** utterly   **c** totally

3 She wore a ___ sunhat.

   a yellow, tiny, spotted   **b** spotted, yellow, tiny   **c** tiny, yellow, spotted

4 Let's book into this ___ inn.

   a lovely, little, traditional   **b** traditional, lovely, little   **c** little, traditional, lovely

5 We had a ___ good time in Madeira.

   a fairly   **b** completely   **c** totally

6 It was ___ freezing when we got to the slopes.

   a extremely   **b** utterly   **c** very

B Complete the text with these adjectives or adverbs.

> absolutely decorated Dutch fully new rather velvet wonderful

Floriade Festival and Bulbfields

Barlinnie Travel, one of Scotland's most reputable tour operators, has an absolutely **(1)** _____ cruise on offer for travellers this spring. Board an impressive, **(2)** _____ luxury liner at Hull harbour and set sail for Venlo in the Netherlands. Cruisers will disembark in Venlo and find themselves in the midst of a spring sensation: the Floriade Festival. **(3)** '_____ fabulous' is how previous visitors to the largest European horticultural exhibition describe the Floriade. But the festival isn't only about beautiful, multi-coloured **(4)** _____ tulips. Held every decade, the festival also presents a **(5)** _____ interesting cultural programme including music, dance, theatre, visual arts and literature. This six-day cruise is **(6)** _____ escorted with English-speaking guides. Prices include transfer to and from the port, six nights full-board and accommodation in an en-suite cabin tastefully **(7)** _____ with lovely, red, **(8)** _____ fabrics, as well as a welcome drink at the Captain's table.

Use your English

A Circle the correct words.

1 Uncle Jim is **in / on / within** a luxury cruise around the Bahamas at the moment.

2 Is there a doctor **in / on / by** board the ship?

3 We travelled south **in / on / within** search of sun, sea and sand.

4 Fortunately, there was a chemist **in / on / at** walking distance of our hotel.

5 Our team came **by / on / within** five points of winning the match.

6 I really hate having to stand **in / at / within** line at airports.

B Now complete the *Exam Task*.

For questions **1 – 12**, choose the answer (**a, b, c** or **d**) which you think fits best according to the text.

Holiday accommodation with a difference

Do you usually (**1**) ___ ordinary hotels that don't seem to have any character? Are you sick (**2**) ___ the same standard of accommodation no matter where you go? If you would (**3**) ___ try something a bit different this year, then head for the West Usk Lighthouse. It's a bed and (**4**) ___ like no other. The Lighthouse, which is located at the point (**5**) ___ the Welsh rivers Usk and Severn meet, once operated as a real lighthouse. Today, it has been transformed into holiday accommodation. The Lighthouse once stood on its own (**6**) ___ an island, but it is now connected with the mainland. However, it is still rather (**7**) ___. If you don't have a private or hired car, you'll have to get around on (**8**) ___ as there are no bus stops or train stations within walking (**9**) ___. There is also a lack (**10**) ___ noisy entertainment facilities in the general area. The most noise you'll hear will be the waves crashing against the rocks in the cove or cows mooing in the nearby fields. This makes it the perfect (**11**) ___ for those who are in (**12**) ___ of a bit of peace and quiet.

1	**a** book into	**b**	check in	**c**	check out	**d**	set off
2	**a** with	**b**	in	**c**	by	**d**	of
3	**a** prefer	**b**	to	**c**	rather	**d**	better
4	**a** inn	**b**	guesthouse	**c**	breakfast	**d**	hostel
5	**a** when	**b**	which	**c**	that	**d**	where
6	**a** in	**b**	on	**c**	to	**d**	at
7	**a** remote	**b**	abroad	**c**	overseas	**d**	distant
8	**a** boat	**b**	board	**c**	foot	**d**	cruise
9	**a** pace	**b**	encounter	**c**	destination	**d**	distance
10	**a** off	**b**	over	**c**	of	**d**	in
11	**a** bay	**b**	retreat	**c**	vessel	**d**	lagoon
12	**a** search	**b**	line	**c**	shuttle	**d**	plan

C For questions **1 – 8**, complete the second sentence so that it has a similar meaning to the first sentence, using the word given. Do not change the word given. You must use between two and five words, including the word given.

1 I have never seen a hotel as beautiful as this!
the
This is _____ I have ever seen.

2 Why can't we go to Paris in the spring?
only
If _____ to Paris in the spring!

3 Living on an island isn't so strange for Dave anymore.
getting
Dave _____ living on an island.

4 Please don't look inside my suitcase.
rather
I'd _____ look inside my suitcase.

5 Benidorm in Spain used to be more popular.
as
Benidorm in Spain _____ it used to be.

6 I should have gone on the guided tour.
had
I _____ on the guided tour.

7 You should not pack all of your clothes under any circumstances.
no
Under _____ pack all of your clothes.

8 He had just dived into the pool when he realised he was still wearing his glasses.
sooner
No _____ into the pool than he realised he was still wearing his glasses.

Writing: a story (2)

Learning Reminder

Prompts & Tenses

- Before you begin writing a story, read and analyse the task very carefully. Work out what kind of emotion the prompt generates and respond to it effectively. Keep this emotion in mind as you write.
- A successful story will make good use of narrative tenses to show the sequence in which events happened in the past. If possible, use the flashback technique to narrate events which happened before the event in the prompt.

A Read the writing task below and then answer the questions below.

You have decided to enter an international short story competition. The competition rules say that the story must begin with the words:

> Sitting alone in the departure lounge, little did Bob realise he was about to have a life-changing journey.

Write your **story** in 140–190 words in an appropriate style.

1 What are the key words in the task?
2 What kind of an emotion does the sentence you must use generate?
3 Who will the story be about?
4 Where is Bob and what is he doing at the time of the event in the prompt?
5 Has the main action happened before or will it happen after this event?
6 What could possibly happen after the event in the prompt?

B Now read the model story and complete the gaps with the correct form of these verbs.

answer   apply   arrange   push   quiz   read   think   smile   walk

Sitting alone in the departure lounge, little did Bob realise he was about to have a life-changing journey. Nervously, he **(1)** _____ his notes with questions his interviewers might ask him.

Suddenly, the announcement came for boarding. An elderly gentleman who was eager to board clumsily **(2)** _____ past Bob, knocking the papers to the floor. 'So sorry,' he said. Bob **(3)** _____, but deep down he was angry. As he **(4)** _____ down the aisle, he saw the old man in the seat next to his. 'Oh no, not him again!' he **(5)** _____.

After take-off, the man **(6)** _____ Bob about his notes. Reluctantly, Bob told him about the interview. The man began asking him questions about his previous experience and what he could bring to the job he **(7)** _____ for. Rather than being annoyed, however, Bob confidently **(8)** _____ the questions.

At the end of the flight, the man said 'Enjoy working in Dublin,' with a wink handing Bob a business card. In disbelief, Bob read that the man was the CEO of the company he **(9)** _____ the interview with.

C Read and complete the *Exam Task* below. Don't forget to use the *Useful Expressions* on page 145 of your Student's Book.

Exam Task

You have decided to enter an international short story competition. The competition rules say that the story must begin with the words:

> Exhausted but happy, Anne and Gordon were looking forward to going home.

Write your **story** in 140–190 words in an appropriate style.

▶ Writing Reference p. 181 in Student's Book

Reading

A Read the *Exam Reminder*. What steps should you take to complete this type of task?

_____

B Now complete the *Exam Task*.

Five healthy ways to detox

In the past, when people wanted to lose weight or start eating a bit more healthily they went on a diet. In recent years, the phrase 'go on a diet' has become unpopular with nutritionists. **1** [ ] But, what's the difference between dieting and detoxing?

Well, diets tend to be very strict regarding what you can and can't eat, how much of it you can eat and how many calories and grams of fat you should consume. **2** [ ] This often comes through forcing themselves to stick to a rigid diet sheet. When detoxing, you may also lose weight, but you will also gain several other health benefits. Nasty toxins will be removed from your body, leaving you feeling healthier in general, and you'll be much less susceptible to disease. In fact, if you regularly detox, you're much less likely to suffer from stress and develop heart conditions. Also, many foods which allow the body to detox help us to feel full quicker, meaning that we'll end up eating less than before. **3** [ ] Then here are five easy, healthy steps to follow to guide you on your way.

First up is sugar. No, don't go rushing off to add more to your coffee! It is the enemy of detoxing. Not only should you try to cut down on your sugar intake in coffee and tea, but you should also avoid products that have added sugar. Some breakfast cereals and ready-made fruit juices may seem like healthy choices, but in fact, if you read the label you'll be surprised at how much sugar they contain. Check for ingredients such as 'fructose corn syrup' and 'dextrose' as these are sugar substitutes that create the same problems as sugar. So what is the problem with sugar? Well, basically, sugar raises blood sugar level and sends messages to the brain that you're not full yet. **4** [ ] If you do this regularly, you run the risk of developing heart disease.

Reducing bad fats is next on the list. The trouble with fat is that, not only does it sit on your hips, but it's also very hard for the digestive system to break it down. While detoxing, avoid fried foods, cheeses and fatty meats. Opt for olive oil, avocados and nuts instead. **5** [ ] The result is you'll eat less at each sitting. But oleic acid also helps to remove toxins from the body as it improves

the digestion of fat. The next time you're feeling peckish, rather than reaching for a high-fat processed snack, have a handful of unsalted nuts instead.

6 [ ] Lean meats like chicken and fresh salmon are excellent sources of protein. If you are vegetarian or vegan, then beans, tofu and whole-grain cereals are packed with protein, as well as being rich in fibre and magnesium. Foods which are rich in protein also help to stabilise your blood sugar level allowing you to feel full for longer.

Also, don't forget high-fibre foods. Oats and beans don't only make you feel full and, therefore, aid weight loss, they can do something quite remarkable. **7** [ ] Try to eat two foods that are high in fibre per serving to boost your system.

Finally, how you eat is just as important as what you eat. Failing to chew properly means that you make your digestive system work much harder. So chew away and let your mouth do all the hard work – you're guaranteed to eat less than you would normally. Put your fork down between each bite and you'll give your brain a chance to register that your stomach is full so you won't keep stuffing it till it reaches bursting point.

Even if you don't want to lose weight, you owe it to yourself to detox from time to time. **8** [ ] But it's the long term benefits, like reduced risk of obesity and heart attacks, that make detoxing a must.

Eight sentences have been removed from the article. Choose from the sentences **A – I** the one which fits each gap
(**1 – 8**). There is one extra sentence which you do not need to use.

A Are you ready to give detoxing a go?

B These are extremely healthy alternatives as they contain oleic acid which helps to curb hunger.

C As a result, you might keep on eating and eating.

D They aid detoxification by pulling cholesterol out of your bloodstream so it is broken down by the
digestive system.

E Today, they recommend that we detox instead.

F The five simple steps above will have you feeling much healthier immediately.

G Upping your protein intake is also essential for detoxing.

H The goal of dieters is to lose weight.

I The problem is that once you stop dieting, the weight get piles back on again.

Vocabulary

A Complete the sentences with the correct form of the word.

1 I got my _____ when I was 13.
2 Did the doctor write a _____ for you?
3 Watch out! That snake's _____!
4 Amy's _____ to nuts.
5 Pomegranates are very _____ for you.
6 Stan's being kept in hospital for an _____.

BRACE
PRESCRIBE
POISON
ALLERGY
BENEFIT
OPERATE

B Complete the words in the sentences.

1 Some people are a _ _ _ _ _ _ _ to antibiotics.
2 Potatoes and pasta are high in c _ _ _ _ _ _ _ _ _ _ _.
3 You'll lose weight in no time on a high f _ _ _ _ diet.
4 Try to w_ _ _ out a few times a week.
5 Vitamins and m _ _ _ _ _ _ _ are an important part of a healthy diet.
6 Rob isn't o _ _ _ _, but he could lose a few pounds.

C Read the text and circle the correct words.

Quinoa – a well-kept Incan secret

The Incans have known about it for thousands of years. In the west,
it has become a staple ingredient of the vegetarian diet over the
past decade due to being extremely rich in (**1**) protein / toxins. It is,
of course, quinoa, a tasty grain that makes a nutritious alternative
to meat. A(n) (**2**) natural / balanced diet no longer means meat and
two veg, thanks to this superfood. It's the perfect (**3**) solution / cure
for those who, either through choice or for health reasons, don't eat
meat. Quinoa can be used as a substitute for rice or pasta for a tasty
(**4**) filling / plentiful meal, which has a slightly (**5**) bitter / crunchy, but
nutty taste. Even those who (**6**) benefit / suffer from gluten allergies
can consume quinoa without fear. Containing all eight of the
(**7**) essential / physical amino acids our bodies need, it's easy to see
why the Incans called it 'the mother of all grains'. So next time you're
trying to decide whether to buy couscous, rice or bulgur wheat for
your favourite salad, (**8**) opt for / warm up quinoa instead. It'll make
a pleasant, nutritious change.

Grammar

Wish & If only; Had better & It's (about/high) time; Would prefer, Prefer & Would rather

A Circle the correct words.

1 I wish I can / could stick to this diet!
2 It's about time we join / joined a gym.
3 If only I hadn't broken / didn't break my leg.
4 Joseph would rather he suffered / suffer than ask the doctor for a prescription.

5 I would prefer to eat / eating at this raw food restaurant.
6 We had better tell / to tell Judy that Rob's off sick.
7 Dimitra prefers to play / playing volleyball to watching TV.
8 It's high time you to start / started eating fruit and vegetables.

B Complete the sentences with the correct form of these words.

book   drink   do   go   not be   open   take   tell

1 I wish I _____ scuba-diving lessons last year.
2 They would prefer _____ into a health spa this year.
3 If only this gym _____ so expensive!
4 He'd better _____ the coach he can't make it to practice tonight.

5 I prefer _____ fruit smoothies to eating fresh fruit.
6 Mum would prefer _____ jogging than to do a team sport.
7 Would you rather _____ an active job or a sedentary one?
8 It's high time they _____ a sports centre in our area.

Listening

A Read the *Exam Reminder*. What should you remember to do before listening?

_____

B 12.1 ▶ Now complete the *Exam Task*.

Exam Reminder

Conquering the exam

- Before listening, remember to read through all of the questions and think of words which you might expect to hear.
- Don't forget to carefully check through all of your answers!

Exam Task

You will hear people talking in eight different situations. For questions **1 – 8**, choose the best answer (**a, b** or **c**).

1 You hear two friends talking about one of them being ill. What has the man taken for his sore throat so far?
   a cough syrup and herbal tea
   b herbal tea and cough sweets
   c cough syrup and cough sweets

2 You hear two friends talking about fitness. How will the woman try to get fit?
   a by going to the gym
   b by joining a dance class
   c by cycling

3 You hear a couple talking about breakfast. What do the couple usually have for breakfast?
   a cereal
   b wholewheat toast
   c fruit smoothies

4 You overhear two friends talking about another friend. What does Carrie look like now?
   a She still has braces.
   b She doesn't have braces or glasses anymore.
   c She still has glasses.

5 You will hear two friends talking about losing weight. How much does the man weigh now?
   a 190 pounds
   b 170 pounds
   c 155 pounds

6 You hear a lady talking to a sports teacher. What has happened?
   a a student has fainted
   b a student has fallen down the stairs
   c a student has fallen into the swimming pool

7 You hear a conversation at someone's house. Which fruit is the woman allergic to?
   a oranges
   b bananas
   c pomegranate

8 You hear a lady talking to her husband about his visit to the doctors. What shouldn't the man do?
   a rest
   b take medication
   c eat healthily

C 12.1 ▶ Listen again and check your answers.

Grammar

Be used to & Get used to; Inversion

A Complete the text by writing one word in each gap.

AcroYoga

Yogi Baba Hari Dass once said, 'Work honestly, meditate every day, meet people without fear and play.' Jason Nemer and Jenny Sauer-Klein, the founders of AcroYoga have definitely found a great way to do all these things at once. Not (1) _____ does AcroYoga demand a great deal of concentration, but also that partners work in complete unison with each other and have fun. AcroYoga has to be seen to be believed. As its name suggests, it's a mixture of yoga and acrobatics. In the past, yoga (2) _____ to be thought of as an activity people did on their own or in a class where yogis were encouraged to focus only on themselves. (3) _____ no circumstances were they allowed to disturb those around them. Those who have been taught more traditional styles of yoga, had better get used (4) _____ AcroYoga, which promotes collaboration between participants. (5) _____ you decide to join an AcroYoga class, you are guaranteed to see the world from a different perspective – or many different perspectives. With the help of your partner, you will find yourself dangling upside down in the most mind-boggling positions known as therapeutic flying. Never (6) _____ yoga been so much fun. (7) _____ did Jason and Jenny realise that what started out as a game for them, would become so popular worldwide. Currently there are over 120 certified AcroYoga teachers worldwide. No (8) _____ had Jason and Jenny created this new style of yoga, than a new group of yogis were eager to join in.

B Choose the correct words.

1 I soon ___ to eating high-fibre foods.
  a was used   **b** got used   **c** used

2 Never ___ been so disappointed as when he lost the tennis match.
  a was he   **b** he had   **c** had he

3 Little ___ how ill she was becoming.
  a did she notice   **b** she did notice   **c** she noticed

4 Under no circumstances ___ them your secret recipe.
  a I will tell   **b** will I tell   **c** do I tell

5 The athletes ___ to such a humid climate, so they couldn't train.
  a weren't used   **b** didn't use   **c** got used

6 ___ once did they offer to help us.
  a No   **b** Never   **c** Not

7 No sooner had the match ended ___ the player collapsed on the pitch.
  a then   **b** that   **c** than

8 Not only can you do aerobics here, ___ you can also do pilates.
  a but   **b** however   **c** also

Use your English

A For questions 1 – 12, read the text below and think of the word which best fits each gap. Use only one word in each gap.

Table tennis champ – a youth inspiration

Darius Knight is an unusual teenager. He would (1) _____ to play table tennis than hang out with his friends. Darius, who (2) _____ to spend his free time on the streets in a gang of 15, realised early on in life that the streets weren't for him. (3) _____ did he realise the first time he went to a table tennis class that his life was about to change forever. When he saw that most of his gang friends started turning to a life of crime, he told himself he (4) _____ better channel his energies in a (5) _____ positive direction. That's when he discovered table tennis. No sooner had he taken up the sport (6) _____ he realised he had found what he had been in search (7) _____. Darius made (8) _____ the top in the sport and has become the British Under-21 National Champion three times as (9) _____ as the European Youth Champion. The teenager is (10) _____ used to being number one in the sport and now has his sights set on adult titles when he comes of age. Not (11) _____ does he want national titles, (12) _____ he also wants to compete internationally. His biggest dream is to win gold in the 2012 Olympics in London.

B For questions 1 – 10, read the text below. Use the word given in capitals at the end of some of the lines to form a word that fits in the gap in the same line.

As you hit the teenage years it's (1) _____ that your body starts to change. You might suddenly find you're putting on weight and don't have much energy. So what's the (2) _____ to make sure you stay in shape during this important stage in your development? You will certainly find a regular programme of physical activity (3) _____.

Most fitness (4) _____ make the (5) _____ that teens do moderate aerobic activity such as walking for one hour a day, and three times per week that they do muscle and bone strengthening activities like gymnastics or football. (6) _____ is another important (7) _____ to good health and staying in shape. Make sure your diet is (8) _____ in vitamins and minerals that help you grow. Don't become too (9) _____ on carbohydrates and high-fat foods for energy.

In a nutshell: eat (10) _____ and keep on the move and you'll manage to stay in shape throughout your teens and into adulthood.

NATURE

SOLVE

BENEFIT

ADVISE
RECOMMEND

NUTRITIOUS
CONTRIBUTE
PLENTY
DEPEND

SENSIBLE

C For questions 1 – 6, complete the second sentence so that it has a similar meaning to the first sentence, using the word given. Do not change the word given. You must use between two and five words, including the word given.

1 You should not ring the bell under any circumstances.
   no
   Under _____ the bell.

2 He had just dived into the pool when he realised he was still wearing his glasses.
   sooner
   No _____ into the pool than he realised he was still wearing his glasses.

3 She had no idea the teacher was angry with her.
   little
   _____ the teacher was angry with her.

4 If only he had kept practising his French, he would still be able to speak it.
   had
   _____ he would still be able to speak it.

5 I have never been so tired after a holiday!
   never
   _____ after a holiday!

6 You are not allowed to touch the food until the guests arrive.
   circumstances
   _____ to touch the food until the guests arrive.

writing: a review

A Read the writing task below and answer the questions.

You recently saw this notice in an English-language magazine called *Your Health*.

Reviews needed!

Have you been to a health spa lately? If so, could you write us a review about it? Include information on the facilities, the staff and the prices and say whether you would recommend the spa to other people. The best reviews will be published next month.

Write your **review** in 140–190 words in an appropriate style.

1 What do you have to write about?
2 What aspects should the review focus on?
3 What facilities might there be at a health spa?
4 Should the review be positive or negative?
5 Who are you writing the review for?

B **Read the model review and decide which paragraphs best complete the gap. Why is this the best choice?**

1
  a I was disappointed by the staff, however. They were friendly enough, but seemed to lack experience. One of the fitness instructors even insulted a client during a fitness class.
  b Regarding the staff, I was really impressed by how welcome they made everyone feel. I truly felt that I was in good hands the whole time and came out feeling extremely pampered.
  c What I enjoyed most was the snack bar. It was well-stocked with lots of tasty, but healthy goodies. I even bought some to take home with me.

2
  d Although a bit expensive, I'd definitely recommend Laurel Health Spa. You're sure to have a relaxing day out.
  e Don't bother going to the spa unless you've got loads of cash to spend. Even then, you could easily find better things to spend it on.
  f I highly recommend Laurel Health Spa. There's nothing I could pick fault with. All in all, a wonderful place to relax.

Laurel Health Spa – the secret of relaxation

It was my first visit to a health spa, so I wasn't sure what to expect. After a day at the Laurel Health Spa in Aby Estate, Newton, I'm hooked for life!

Set in the calmest country surroundings imaginable, the spa is amazingly well equipped. The three spotless swimming pools – one outdoors, Jacuzzi and Turkish baths were more than I had expected. What I liked most, though, was the Indian head massage I received in the massage parlour. Not to be missed! There are also classes in pilates and tai chi for those who are feeling energetic.

(1) ___

The only thing that I didn't find impressive was the cost. General entrance is fairly reasonable at £30, but be careful, this doesn't cover massages or fitness classes. Be warned and take extra cash.

(2) ___

C **Read and complete the *Exam Task* below. Don't forget to use the *Useful Expressions* on page 157 of your Student's Book.**

Exam Task

You recently saw this notice in an English-language magazine called *Your Health*.

Reviews needed!

Have you been to the new sports centre in town yet? If so, could you write us a review about it? Include information on the range of sports on offer, the building and the location and say whether you would recommend the sports centre to other people. The best reviews will be published next month.

Write your **review** in 140–190 words in an appropriate style.

➲ Writing Reference p. 183 in Student's Book

Vocabulary

A **Choose the correct answers.**

1 Are you immune ____ measles?

   a for   **c** from

   b to   **d** on

2 I have a(n) ____ throat and a blocked nose.

   a sore   **c** painful

   b raw   **d** itchy

3 The plane sat on the ____ for an hour before take-off.

   a quay   **c** departure gate

   b dock   **d** runway

4 The ____ entertainment was a comedy film.

   a cabin   **c** in-flight

   b overhead   **d** remote

5 Eating only ____ foods is good for your health.

   a seasonal   **c** processed

   b plentiful   **d** bitter

6 Sharon's trying to reduce her ____ of caffeine.

   a nutrition   **c** cure

   b intake   **d** weight

7 Look! The flight has already ____!

   a cancelled   **c** boarded

   b transferred   **d** declared

8 Let's go ____ round Europe this summer.

   a journey   **c** backpacking

   b tour   **d** backtracking

9 Always ____ up before you do any form of exercise.

   a work   **c** wake

   b warm   **d** fill

10 No lunch for me, thanks – I've lost my ____.

   a appetite   **c** minerals

   b recovery   **d** temperature

11 Mum says I would benefit ____ a break in the sun.

   a with   **c** from

   b to   **d** for

12 ____ should always contain gauze.

   a Stethoscopes   **c** Hot water bottles

   b Contact lenses   **d** First-aid kits

13 How much is the train ____ from Euston to Luton?

   a price   **c** fee

   b fare   **d** payment

14 We arrived at our ____ extremely tired.

   a destination   **c** timetable

   b itinerary   **d** reservation

15 Fran was charged £40 for ____ baggage.

   a duty-free   **c** essential

   b hand   **d** excess

16 The tourists went ____ search of local cuisine.

   a on   **c** at

   b within   **d** in

17 After a week at a country ____, I felt relaxed.

   a retreat   **c** shuttle

   b preservation **d** remedy

18 Get vaccinated against ____ diseases before travelling.

   a poisonous   **c** distant

   b dependent   **d** infectious

19 Let's see if there are any rooms at this ____ .

   a harbour   **c** liner

   b bed and breakfast **d** gulf

20 Will you please wipe your ____ nose?

   a broken   **c** runny

   b catching   **d** obese

21 I like to ____ out in the gym three times a week.

   a check   **c** pull

   b work   **d** figure

22 You shouldn't ____ breakfast, because it's an important meal.

   a jump   **c** leap

   b skip   **d** hop

23 How long were you ____ sea for?

   a on   **c** by

   b in   **d** at

24 She passed ____ in fright at the sight of the shark.

   a out   **c** under

   b off   **d** up

25 I hope you have booked us ____ a nice hotel!

   a up   **c** over

   b into   **d** in

26 When did you come ____ with this cold?

   a down   **c** over

   b up   **d** across

27 It's a long way to walk, but it's ____ cycling distance.

   a in   **c** within

   b with   **d** on

28 Call a doctor. I'm ____ agony.

   a under   **c** in

   b with   **d** on

Grammar

B Choose the correct answers.

1 Under no circumstances ___ to that hotel.
 a you should go **c** should you go
 b do you go **d** you go

2 It was the ___ holiday I had ever been on.
 a relaxing **c** too relaxing
 b more relaxing **d** most relaxing

3 Kay doesn't want to go skiing. She would rather ___ swimming instead.
 a to go **c** going
 b go **d** prefer going

4 It's about time you ___ up a hobby.
 a took **c** are taking
 b take **d** had taken

5 No sooner had they arrived at the resort ___ it started pouring with rain.
 a than **c** then
 b that **d** and

6 I can't get used ___ by plane.
 a travel **c** travelling
 b to travel **d** to travelling

7 Would you prefer ___ a film instead of a play?
 a to see **c** see
 b seeing **d** we see

8 Rarely ___ go abroad on holiday.
 a do they **c** they will
 b they **d** have they

9 Not once ___ to take me to the gym.
 a does she offer **c** has she offered
 b she has offered **d** she offers

10 You had better ___ with a trusted travel agent.
 a booking **c** with booking
 b to book **d** book

11 I'd rather ___ a photo of me in my bikini!
 a not take **c** didn't take
 b you didn't take **d** didn't you take

12 Put on your ___ gloves if you're going jogging.
 a warm, grey, woollen **c** woollen, grey, warm
 b grey, woollen, warm **d** warm, woollen, grey

13 The ferry is ___ means of transport to get to Italy.
 a slow **c** slowest
 b slower **d** the slowest

14 It's ___ boiling in Cairo at this time of the year.
 a extremely **c** very
 b absolutely **d** slightly

15 ___ did I realise the holiday was going to end in disaster.
 a Little **c** Not only
 b Rarely **d** No sooner

16 The beach is not as crowded ___ we expected it to be.
 a as **c** than
 b so **d** more

17 I wish I ___ on a desert island.
 a am **c** will be
 b have been **d** was

18 Lucy used ___ as a tour rep.
 a to work **c** to working
 b working **d** with working

19 No sooner had they booked the tickets, than ___ planning their next holiday.
 a did they start **c** they start
 b they started **d** they have started

20 Look at that ___ sports car.
 a Italian, red, beautiful **c** red, Italian, beautiful
 b red, beautiful, Italian **d** beautiful, red, Italian

21 I'm not as sporty ___ you.
 a as **c** than
 b like **d** for

22 You ___ ask your mother about this.
 a would better **c** are better
 b had better **d** have better

23 'You look exhausted.' 'I'm not ___ up so late.'
 a used to staying **c** getting used to stay
 b used to stay **d** getting to stay

24 If only he ___ about the new rules.
 a knows **c** had known
 b is knowing **d** have known

25 The further he ran, the ___ he became.
 a more tired **c** most tired
 b tireder **d** tiredest

26 The film was ___ good.
 a absolutely **c** utterly
 b totally **d** extremely

27 Do you like my ___ bag?
 a blue new school **c** new school blue
 b new blue school **d** blue school new

28 'Shall we go out?' 'I ___ stay in.'
 a 'd rather **c** 'm rather
 b 've rather **d** 'll rather